Sew Special
Fat Quarter Gifts™

HOUSE of
WHITE
BIRCHES

PUBLISHERS
SINCE 1947

Sew Special
Fat Quarter Gifts™

Editor Julie Johnson
Art Director Brad Snow
Publishing Services Director Brenda Gallmeyer

Managing Editor Dianne Schmidt
Assistant Art Director Nick Pierce
Copy Supervisor Michelle Beck
Copy Editors Nicki Lehman, Mary O'Donnell, Renée Wright
Technical Editor Marla Freeman

Graphic Arts Supervisor Ronda Bechinski
Graphic Artists Glenda Chamberlain, Edith Teegarden
Production Assistants Marj Morgan, Judy Neuenschwander
Technical Artist Nicole Gage

Photography Supervisor Tammy Christian
Photography Matthew Owen
Photo Stylist Tammy Steiner

Printed in China
First Printing: 2009
Library of Congress Control Number: 2008901109
Hardcover ISBN: 978-1-59217-219-1

DRGbooks.com

1 2 3 4 5 6 7 8 9

Create, Sew & Give!

What better way to celebrate life than to create and give special handcrafted gifts—gifts created with the user in mind, designed for dear family members and friends, to show how special they are.

A very special time in our lives is the birth of a child or grandchild. But special little packages have special needs: baby quilts, changing pads, diaper bags and bibs. As our children grow, it's so nice to quilt simple, snugly blankets for sleepy times, and sew crayon caddies and aprons for creative times.

Give the comforts of home to those dear to us who are far away. Whether you want to quilt a special comforter, create an adorable dorm-room pillow set or a lap-warmer for an aging parent, you'll find special home comforts in this chapter.

Some girls just want to have fun. What better gift than a pretty bag for that special girl to let her have fun wherever she goes? Create simple-to-sew totes, purses, jewelry rolls and unique gift bags with that special girl in mind. Remember, the young at heart are never too old to enjoy a new bag!

Celebrations with family and friends are often centered around dining and comfort foods, so you'll want to gift special creations keeping the heart of the home in mind. Whether you need to stitch up a special casserole cover, want to stop over for a "cuppa java," or simply want to dress the table for each season, you'll find insightful, thoughtful gifts that say "you're special to me" in this section.

Our last chapter of gifts to sew is simply that: last-minute gifts that are for those very special occasions when you just run out of time. These gifts are meant to be simple but special. They are easy and inexpensive to sew, but still show how much you care. Whether the gift is for a book lover, a special sewing friend or a chef, you'll find delightful last-minute gifts in this chapter.

So take some time to create these beautiful gifts sewn with love from your heart. Fashion fat quarter gifts by sewing and quilting charming fabric 18 x 22-inch rectangles into unique gifts for everyone on your gift list.

Create, sew and give, and enjoy the celebration of life.

Julie

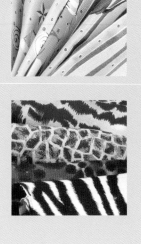

Contents

Sew Sweet Baby

Comforts of Home

Bags & More

Heart of the Home

Last-Minute Gifts

Sew Sweet Baby

Sewing for the baby is a time-honored tradition women enjoy with each new generation. Whether your new arrival needs a baby-changing station, a sleepy-time quilt and diaper bag, or a special-occasion bib, you'll love sewing the designs in this chapter for your special little bundle of joy. And the fun only continues as needs change to crayon caddies and aprons for toddlers.

Stitched With Love Quilt & Tote

Designs by Carolyn Vagts

Use pretty batik fabrics for a simple block baby quilt and matching tote. This quilt is sure to please any young mother.

Finished sizes
Quilt: 46 x 58 inches
Tote: 12¼ x 9½ x 2 inches

Materials
- Fat quarters lightweight
  woven fabric:
    6 peach
    6 lavender
- 44/45-inch-wide lightweight
  woven fabric:
    ¼ yard peach
    ½ yard lavender
    3 yards for quilt backing
    ¾ yard for tote lining and pocket
- Batting:
    52 x 64 inches for quilt
    25 x 35 inches for tote
- Basic sewing supplies and equipment

Quilt

Cutting

Note: Reserve fat-quarter scraps for tote.

From peach fat quarters:
- Cut 16 (2½ x 20-inch) strips.
- Cut 24 (6⅞ x 6⅞-inch) squares. Cut each square in half diagonally.
- Cut four 4 x 4-inch squares for corners.

From lavender fat quarters:
- Cut 16 (2½ x 20-inch) strips.
- Cut 24 (6⅞ x 6⅞-inch) squares. Cut each square in half diagonally.

From ¼ yard peach fabric:
- Cut five 1½-inch strips the width of the fabric for first border.

From ½ yard lavender fabric:
- Cut six 2½-inch strips the width of the fabric for binding.

Assembly

Use ¼-inch seam allowance unless otherwise stated. Sew right sides together. Press seams as you sew.

1. Sew one peach and one lavender half-square triangle together along the diagonal cut. Press seam open. Repeat to make a total of 48 blocks.

2. Lay out blocks into groups of four with all the peach sections on the inside (Figure 1). Sew the top two blocks together, then the bottom two, then sew the top and bottom units together to make 12 block units. Press.

Figure 1

3. Referring to Figure 2, arrange block units in four rows of three units each. Sew three units

together to make a row, then sew rows together to complete center of quilt.

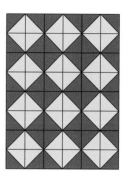

Figure 2

4. Sew peach borders to top and bottom of center, then sew to sides (Figure 3), piecing strips as needed and trimming to fit.

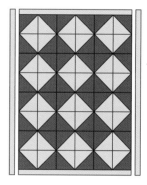

Figure 3

5. Sew four of the 2½ x 20-inch strips together along the 20-inch sides, alternating peach and lavender to make 8 groups of 8½ x 20-inch units. Press. Crosscut units into 24 (4-inch) sections (Figure 4). *Note: Remainder of units will be used for tote.*

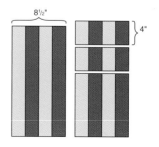

Figure 4

6. Sew five pieced units together to make the top border (Figure 5). Repeat to make the bottom border. Remove one end unit. Sew in place.

Figure 5

7. Sew seven pieced units together to make each side unit; remove three end units, and sew a 4-inch corner square to each end (Figure 6). Sew in place.

Figure 6

8. Layer batting between quilt top and backing fabric. Pin or baste together. Trim layers even. Quilt as desired.

9. Join binding strips diagonally and trim seam allowance (Figure 7). Press binding in half along length with wrong sides together. Unfold one

end and trim it at a 45-degree angle, then turn under the edge ½ inch. Refold and press it back again (Figure 8).

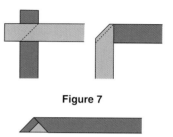

Figure 7

Figure 8

10. With right sides together and raw edges even, sew binding around quilt using a ¼-inch seam allowance, beginning at the center of one side and stitching until ¼ inch from the first corner. Angle the sewing direction to a 45-degree angle and sew off to the corner point (Figure 9).

Stop ¼"

Figure 9

11. Fold binding strip up and away from the quilt, then fold it back into place along the next side to be stitched. The fold should be even with the raw edges of the first side just stitched (Figure 10). Continue stitching to next corner. Repeat to finish sides.

Figure 10

12. Trim end of binding so it can be tucked inside the pocket at the beginning of the binding, and finish stitching the seam. Turn the folded edge of the binding over the raw edges and to the back of the quilt. Hand-stitch binding in place.

Assembly

Use ¼-inch seam allowance unless otherwise stated. Sew right sides together. Press seams as you sew.

1. Sew one peach and one lavender half-square triangle together along the diagonal cut. Press seam open. Repeat to make a total of 16 blocks.

2. Referring to Figure 1 of Quilt Assembly, lay out blocks into groups of four with all the peach sections on the inside. Sew the top two blocks together, then the bottom two, then sew the top and bottom units together to make 4 block units. Press.

3. Sew two units together (Figure 11). Repeat with remaining two units. These are the centers for the front and back of the tote.

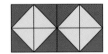

Figure 11

4. Sew a 12½ x 1½-inch strip to the top and bottom of each unit. Sew an 8½ x 1½-inch strip to each side of each unit (Figure 12).

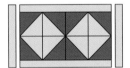

Figure 12

5. Sew a 14½ x 2½-inch strip across the bottom of the front and the back, and sew a 10½ x 2½-inch strip to the right side of each unit (Figure 13).

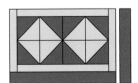

Figure 13

Tote

Cutting

From peach fat quarters:
- Cut eight 3⅞ x 3⅞-inch squares. Cut each square in half diagonally to make 16 triangles.

- Cut four 12½ x 1½-inch strips.

- Cut four 8½ x 1½-inch strips.

From lavender fat quarters:
- Cut eight 3⅞ x 3⅞-inch squares. Cut each square in half diagonally to make 16 triangles.

- Cut two 14½ x 2½-inch strips.

- Cut two 10½ x 2½-inch strips.

From remaining 4-section units (Step 5 of Quilt):
- Cut four 8½ x 2½-inch sections for top band.

- Cut eight 8½ x 4½-inch sections for handles.

From fabric for tote lining and pocket:
- Cut one 33 x 12½-inch rectangle for pocket.

From batting:
- Cut one 33 x 12½-inch rectangle for tote.

- Cut one 33 x 6½-inch rectangle for pocket.

- Cut two 2 x 32-inch strips for handles.

6. Sew both units together to make one long unit (Figure 14).

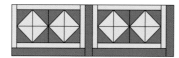

Figure 14

7. Sew the 2½-inch 4-section units together to make a strip and sew across the top of the unit (Figure 15). Trim 4-section unit to fit pieced tote unit. Use pieced unit as a pattern to cut lining fabric. Set lining aside.

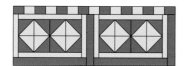

Figure 15

8. Pin-baste batting to the wrong side of the joined unit and stitch in the ditch around blocks and borders to quilt.

9. Fold pocket rectangle in half with right sides together. Layer the 33 x 6½-inch piece of batting on one side and stitch through all thicknesses along long raw edges. Turn pocket rectangle right side out with batting sandwiched between. Press. Topstitch along seamed (top) edge (Figure 16).

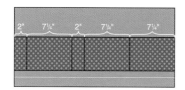

Figure 16

10. Position pocket on right side of lining with bottom of pocket 2½ inches from bottom of lining. Topstitch across bottom edge of pocket. Make vertical stitches to divide pocket (Figure 17).

Figure 17

11. Sew four handle strips together to make one 32½-inch-long unit. Repeat with remaining four handle strips. Press each unit in half with right sides together, matching long edges. Layer a strip of batting on one side and sew along the long raw edges of each unit through all thicknesses. Turn handles right side out. Press.

12. Referring to Handle Placement Diagram, baste ends of handles to top edge of tote. Sew lining and tote with right sides together across top edge, catching ends of handles in stitching.

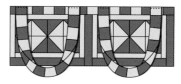

Stitched With Love Quilt & Tote
Handle Placement Diagram

13. With right sides together and handles inside, fold tote and lining in half, matching sides. Stitch across bottom and side of tote, and across side and bottom of lining, leaving an opening in bottom of lining for turning.

Figure 18

14. Fold the bottom of the tote, matching the bottom seam with the side seams, and stitch across the bottom 1 inch from the points (Figure 18). Trim seam allowance. Repeat for the lining. Turn the tote and lining right side out. Hand-stitch the lining opening closed and fit lining into tote. Topstitch around top edge of tote. ⊗

Sweet Baby Quilt

Design by Connie Kauffman

A baby quilt for a special baby is a thoughtful gift for the new mother and child. Use pretty pastels in neutral colors for a soft, sweet look.

Finished size
32 x 37 inches

Materials
• 5 cotton fat quarters:
  1 light baby print
  1 pink print
  1 violet print
  1 yellow print
  1 pastel blue print
• 44/45-inch-wide lightweight cotton fabric:
  ¾ yard light yellow print
  1⅛ yards pastel pink print for backing
• 38 x 43 inches batting
• Multicolored cotton thread
• Basic sewing supplies and equipment

Cutting
From five cotton fat quarters:
  • Cut four 5½ x 5½-inch squares from each.

  • Cut five 2½ x 5½-inch rectangles each from four fat quarters and four 2½ x 5½-inch rectangles from the remaining fat quarter.

From ¾ yard light yellow print:
  • Cut two 2½ x 24½-inch strips for inner top and bottom borders.

- Cut two 2½ x 25½-inch strips for inner side borders.

- Cut two 2½ x 32½-inch strips for outer top and bottom borders.

- Cut two 2½ x 33½-inch strips for outside borders.

- Cut four 2-inch strips the width of the fabric for binding.

Assembly

Use ¼-inch seam allowance. Sew with right sides together, unless otherwise stated. Press seams as you sew.

1. Refer to Assembly Diagram to sew 5½ x 5½-inch blocks into five rows of four blocks each. Sew rows together to make center of quilt.

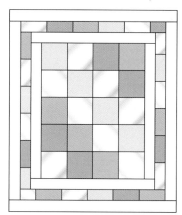

Sweet Baby Quilt
Assembly Diagram

2. Sew inner side borders to sides of pieced blocks. Sew inner top and bottom borders across top and bottom.

3. Sew short edges of 2½ x 5½-inch rectangles to make a top, a bottom, and two side pieced border strips of six rectangles each.

4. Sew side pieced border strips in place. Trim off excess fabric (Figure 1). Repeat for top and bottom pieced border strips.

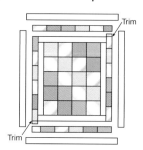

Figure 1

5. Sew on outer side borders and then outer top and bottom borders.

6. Sandwich batting between backing fabric and pieced top. Quilt as desired using multicolored cotton thread. Trim edges of layers even.

7. Sew binding strips together and fold in half lengthwise, wrong sides together. Sew to right side of quilt with raw edges even. Fold binding to wrong side of quilt and hand-stitch or stitch-in-the-ditch folded edge to quilt. ⊗

Sources: Batting from Hobbs Bonded Fibers; Blendables thread from Sulky of America.

Baby Announcement Board

Design by Connie Kauffman

This small wall hanging is a great way to display baby's first photo and announcement. This quilt can be made with four fat quarters. Embellishments are fun to add to this project with letter beads, buttons, ribbons, etc. This would be a great gift to a mother, grandmother, aunt or close family friend.

Finished size
12 x 14½ inches

Materials
• Coordinating cotton fat quarters:
    1 light pink print
    1 medium pink print
    1 dark pink print
    1 blue-and-pink print
• 17 x 15 inches batting
• Baby photo and announcement card
• Beads:
    letter beads to spell Baby's name
    pink or blue beads for spacers
    approximately 20 small pearl beads
• Buttons:
    2 each ¼-inch pink and blue
    4 (½-inch) white
• 6 inches flat lace
• Assorted widths white, pink and blue ribbons in
    varying lengths
• 3 x 3-inch square fusible web
• 2 baby-rattle embellishments
• Basic sewing supplies and equipment

Cutting
From light pink print fat quarter:
• Cut one 12½ x 9-inch (C) rectangle.

• Cut two 3 x 3-inch squares for heart photo tabs.

From medium pink print fat quarter:
• Cut one 12½ x 1¼-inch strip.

From dark pink print fat quarter:
• Cut one 14½ x 12½-inch rectangle for backing.

• Cut one 8 x 5¼-inch (A) rectangle.

• Cut one 12½ x 4½-inch strip for hanging sleeve.

From blue-and-pink print fat quarter:
• Cut one 5 x 5¼-inch (B) rectangle.

• Cut three 2½ x 22-inch strips for binding.

Jenna Grace

January 7, 2006
5:41 a.m.
6 pounds, 0 ounces
21 inches

Assembly

Use ¼-inch seam allowance unless otherwise stated. Press as you sew. Refer to Assembly Diagram.

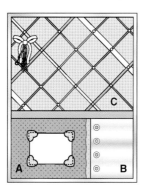

Baby Announcement Board
Assembly Diagram

1. Place dark pink (A) rectangle and blue-and-pink (B) rectangle right sides together. Sandwich 6-inch length of flat lace between rectangles along one short edge. Sew together, catching edge of lace in seam (Figure 1). Press seam so lace lays over dark pink rectangle. Trim lace even with fabric edges.

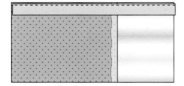

Figure 1

2. With right sides together, sew medium pink strip to top of A/B rectangles (Figure 2). Press seam.

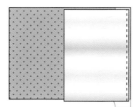

Figure 2

3. Tape 14½ x 12½-inch dark pink backing, right side down, to a flat surface. Lay batting and light pink rectangle (C) on top with right side of rectangle facing up. Pin in place. Crisscross ribbons diagonally across rectangle, spacing 2–2½ inches apart (Figure 3).

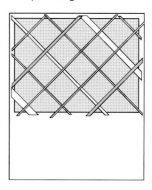

Figure 3

4. Pin ribbons at each intersection and at edges of fabric, making sure ribbon is flat across the entire surface. Remove tape. Carefully remove pins at edges of fabric and tack ribbons in place. Determine placement of photo; remove pins at ribbon intersections underneath photo and tack ribbons in place. Remove each remaining pin one at a time and sew a pearl bead at each ribbon intersection. ***Note:*** *If intersections are close to edges of blocks, temporarily tack in place until binding is on.*

5. Sew the top edge of the medium pink strip to the bottom of the light pink block to attach the bottom pieced blocks (Figure 4). Press seam toward A/B block. Layer quilt with wrong sides together, and quilt batting between. To quilt, stitch in the ditch on the bottom of the medium pink strip and again between the dark pink rectangle and the blue-and-pink rectangle. Quilt along lines of pattern on fabric or as desired in blue-and-pink rectangle.

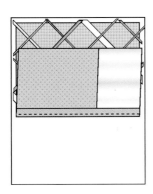

Figure 4

6. Sew binding strips with bias seams; press. Fold binding lengthwise with wrong sides together; press. With raw edges even, sew binding to right side of mat, mitering corners and leaving first 3 inches unstitched. Join end of binding to beginning on the bias and press. Finish stitching.

7. Sew a ¼-inch hem on each short edge of hanging sleeve. With wrong sides together, sew long edges together. Press with seam in middle. Hand-stitch sleeve to top of backing.

8. Follow manufacturer's instructions to use 3 x 3-inch square of fusible web to bond 3 x 3-inch squares of light pink print together. Use template to cut out four heart photo tabs. Position tabs at corners of announcement card on dark pink A block and pin in place. Remove card and stitch tabs in place at points of hearts; slip corners of card into tabs.

9. Thread name beads with spacers onto length of thread and attach to medium pink strip. Sew pink and blue buttons to white buttons, and then attach to blue-and-pink block next to edge of lace. If desired, sew pearl beads to lace as shown.

10. Attach baby rattles to mat with ribbon and embellish with a bow. ⊗

Source: Steam-A-Seam2 fusible web from The Warm Company.

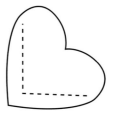

Baby Announcement Board
Heart Photo Tab Template
Actual Size

Baby Block Play Mat

Design by Connie Kauffman

This dresser play mat is a simple quilt accented with fusible appliqué. Using soft pastel fabric in baby print and pastel pink or blue accents, the mat is made from three fat quarters and finished with simple crosshatch quilting.

Finished size
21 x 18 inches

Materials
• Coordinating cotton fat quarters:
    2 pastel baby print
    1 pink or blue print

• 22 x 19 inches batting
• 12 x 12 inches fusible web
• Coordinating variegated all-purpose thread
• Basic sewing supplies and equipment

Instructions

Use ¼-inch seam allowance unless otherwise stated. Press as you sew.

1. Trace appliqué templates (page 22) onto fusible web, reversing pieces as noted on templates. Cut out just outside traced lines. Fuse onto wrong side of pink or blue print fabric and cut out on traced lines. Remove paper backing.

2. Iron pastel baby print fat quarters. Place one fat quarter faceup. Referring to photo for placement, position appliqués on fat quarter so they are at least ½ inch from edge of fabric. Fuse in place following manufacturer's instructions. Stitch around edges of each appliqué using blanket stitch and variegated thread.

3. Place quilt batting on flat surface. Place second baby print fat quarter and appliquéd mat top right sides together on quilt batting. Pin all layers together.

4. Sew around edges of mat, stitching ¼ inch from appliqués across top and bottom, and making a straight seam along the two sides with a 3½-inch opening on one side for turning (Figure 1).

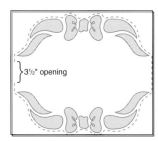

Figure 1

5. Trim seams. Turn mat right side out. Press under seam allowance at opening and hand-stitch closed. Press mat.

6. To quilt, straight-stitch around each appliqué and stitch between appliqués with crosshatch pattern, or as desired. ⊗

Sources: Variegated thread from Sulky of America; Steam-A-Seam2 from The Warm Company; poly-cotton batting from Hobbs Bonded Fibers.

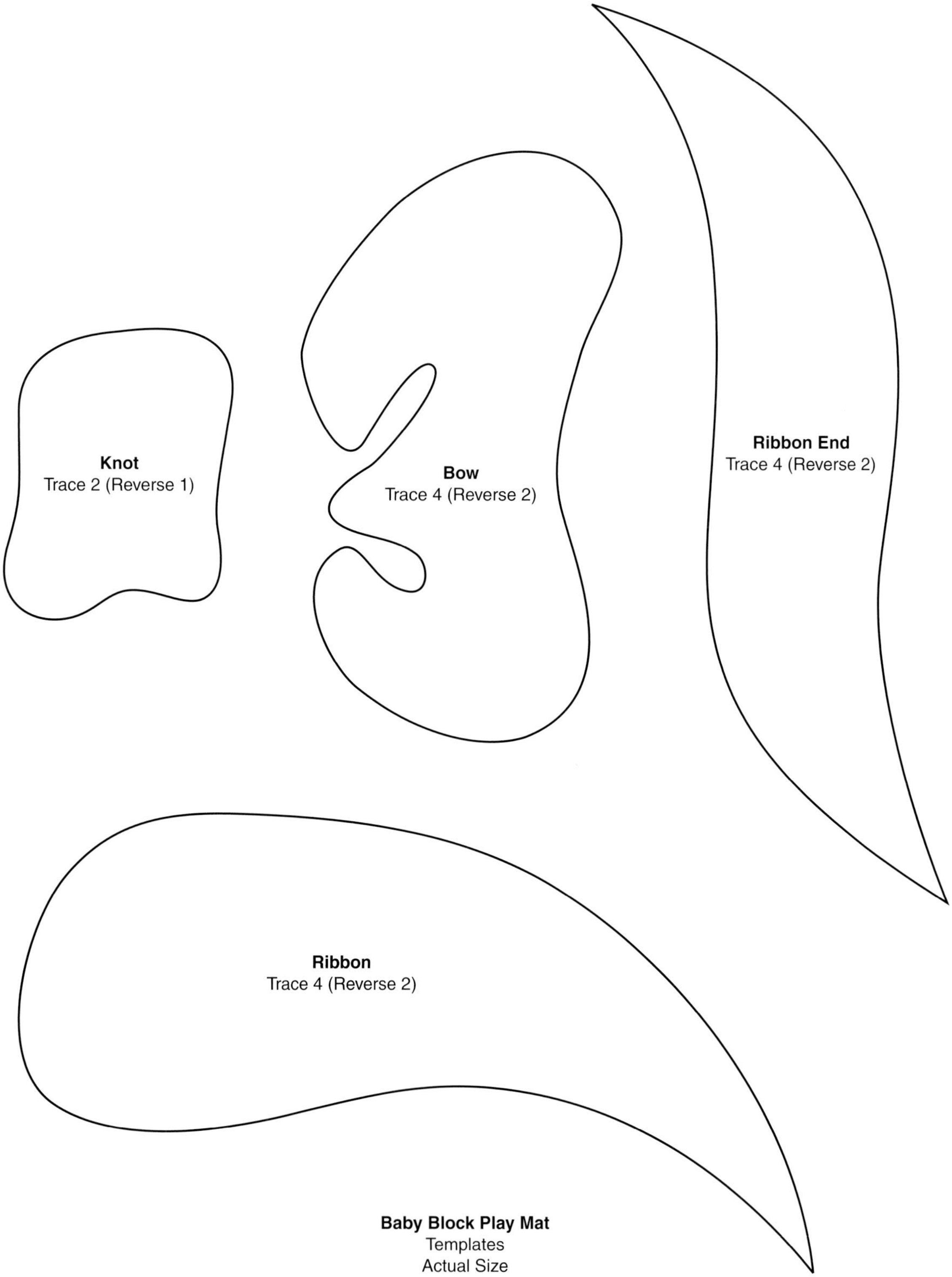

Knot
Trace 2 (Reverse 1)

Bow
Trace 4 (Reverse 2)

Ribbon End
Trace 4 (Reverse 2)

Ribbon
Trace 4 (Reverse 2)

Baby Block Play Mat
Templates
Actual Size

Crayon Caddy

Design by Pamela Hastings

This little caddy is perfect for toting crayons and easily fits into backpacks and purses. Opened, your budding artist can see all the colors of the rainbow at once. When coloring time is over, simply fold, roll and tie with a bow.

Finished size
10 x 10 inches, open

Materials
• 1 fat quarter
• Scrap contrasting fabric
• Bias binding to match contrasting fabric
• Basic sewing supplies and equipment

Cutting
From fat quarter:
• Cut one 16 x 21-inch rectangle for caddy.

From scrap of contrasting fabric:
• Cut two 1¾ x 11-inch strips for binding.

• Cut two 3 x 14-inch strips for ties.

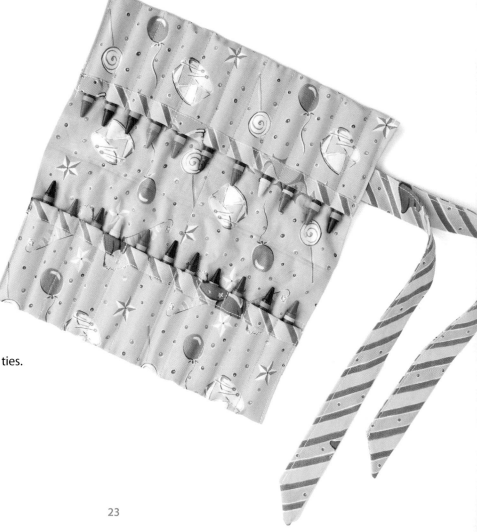

Assembly

Use ½-inch seam allowance unless otherwise stated. Sew with right sides together. Press as you sew.

1. Sew 16-inch edges of caddy rectangle together. Turn right side out and press so seam is in the middle (Figure 1). ***Note:*** *The side with the seam showing will be referred to as the inside from now on.*

Figure 1

2. Finish one long edge of each binding strip with a serger or a zigzag stitch. Pin the right side of one strip to the outside of the caddy on one unfinished end with raw edges even; stitch (Figure 2). Wrap strip over raw edge, turning ends under. Topstitch close to first stitching, catching end on inside of caddy (Figure 3). Repeat on opposite end of caddy with second binding strip.

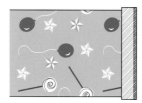   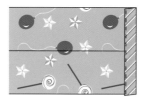

Figure 2   **Figure 3**

3. Turn ends of caddy to inside 3 inches (Figure 4).

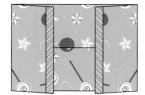

Figure 4

4. Sew each tie in half lengthwise, stitching diagonally at one end and leaving opposite end open. Trim seams. Turn right side out and press. Topstitch.

5. Layer ties together and place between side edges of caddy on one end. Pin sides of caddy in place. Topstitch (Figure 5).

Figure 5

6. Beginning at one side, mark vertical lines every ¾ inch across on both ends. Stitch on marked lines.

7. Insert crayons in pockets. Fold caddy in half and roll toward the ties. Wrap the ends around the caddy and tie in a bow. ⊗

Hugs & Kisses Baby Woobie

Design by Lisa Swenson Ruble

Baby's favorite blanket doesn't have to be big! The hugs and kisses block pattern of this little quilt shows your love for the little one, and the round corner tabs make for easy grabbing as this great woobie becomes a constant companion.

Finished size
22½ x 22½ inches, excluding corner tabs

Materials
- Cotton fat quarters:
    - 1 turquoise mini print
    - 1 blue dot
    - 1 lime mini print
    - 1 yellow dot
    - 2 large dot
- 27 x 27-inch square coordinating solid for backing
- Batting:
    - 27 x 27 inches
    - 18 x 18 inches
- Basic sewing supplies and equipment

Cutting
From turquoise mini print fat quarter:
- Cut four 3 x 22-inch strips. Subcut into 25 (3-inch) squares.

From blue dot fat quarter:
- Cut three 3 x 22-inch strips. Subcut into 20 (3-inch) squares.

From lime mini print fat quarter:
• Cut two 3⅜ x 22-inch strips. Subcut into eight 3⅜-inch squares.

• Cut three 3 x 22-inch strips. Subcut into 16 (3-inch) squares.

From yellow dot fat quarter:
• Cut two 3⅜ x 22-inch strips. Subcut into eight 3⅜-inch squares.

• Cut one 3 x 22-inch strip. Subcut into four 3-inch squares.

From large dot fat quarters:
• Cut eight of template A (page 29).

From 18 x 18-inch batting:
• Cut four of template B (page 29).

Assembly
Use ¼-inch seam allowance. Sew with right sides together, unless otherwise stated. Press seams as you sew.

1. Referring to X Block Assembly Diagram, sew blue dot and turquoise squares together to make five pieced blocks.

2. On the wrong side of 3⅜-inch yellow dot squares, draw diagonal lines from corner to corner (Figure 1). Sew each yellow dot square to a lime mini print square, sewing ¼ inch on each side of the diagonal line (Figure 2). Cut each on the diagonal line to make 16 triangle units (Figure 3). Referring to O Block Assembly Diagram, sew 3-inch yellow dot squares, 3-inch lime mini print squares, and triangle units together to make four pieced blocks.

Figure 1   **Figure 2**

Figure 3

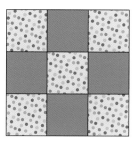

Hugs & Kisses Baby Woobie
X Block Assembly Diagram

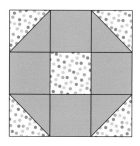

Hugs & Kisses Baby Woobie
O Block Assembly Diagram

3. Using the photo as a guide, sew pieced blocks together as shown.

4. Pair two large dot circles right sides together and sew around edge, leaving an opening as indicated on template. Turn right side out. Press flat. Insert batting circle. Pin in place and quilt as desired. ***Note:*** *Opening will be covered by quilt corners.* Repeat to make a total of four circles.

5. Layer quilt backing and quilt top right sides together on top of batting. Pin layers together. Sew around outer edge, leaving approximately 3 inches at each corner for inserting quilted circles.

6. Trim excess backing and batting. Turn right side out through corner opening. Press under seam allowances at corner openings.

7. Sandwich quilted circles between layers and pin in place. Topstitch edges of quilt ¼ inch from edge. Quilt pieced blocks as desired. ⊗

Source: Isadora Phoenix' Woodstock fabric collection from Benartex.

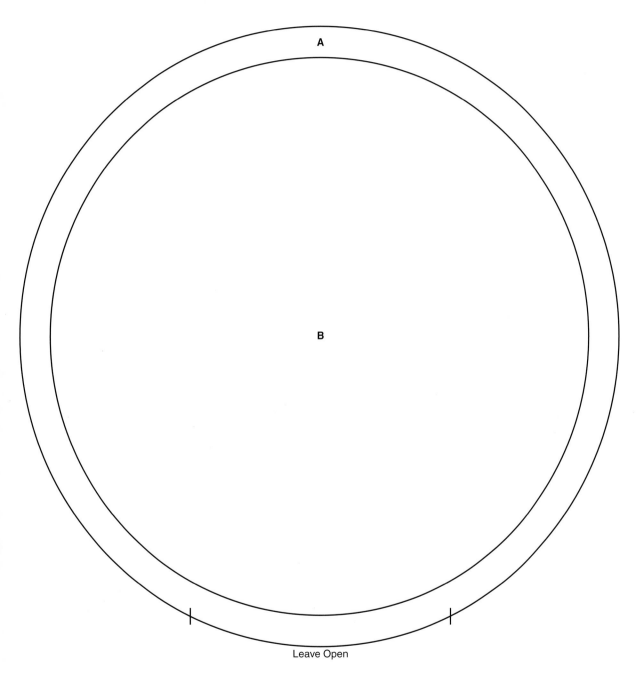

Leave Open

Hugs & Kisses Baby Woobie
Templates
Actual Size

Dots, Flowers & Bows

Designs by Cheryl Stranges

A perfect gift for a new mother is an adorable diaper bag and matching bib made from fat quarters and embellished with special touches of lace and embroidery designs. You'll be surprised how fast it is to make this gift when you use your serger.

Finished sizes
Bag: 20 x 14 x 4 inches, excluding handles
Bib: 16 x 10 inches

Materials
- Coordinating cotton fat quarters:
  2 prints for diaper bag front
    and back
  2 prints for diaper bag pockets
  2 solid color for diaper bag lining
  2 prints for baby bib
- Scrap craft fur
- 34 x 45 inches quilt batting
- 45 inches fusible tricot interfacing
- 2 (16½ x 4-inch) pieces firm interfacing
- Iron-on stabilizer
- Satin ribbon:
  30 inches ¼ inch wide
  20 inches each 2 styles ¾ inch wide
  20 inches 1½ inches wide
  45 inches 2 inches wide
- 5 x 7-inch piece clear vinyl for photo pocket
- 1½ inches ¾-inch-wide hook-and-loop tape
- Optional: embroidery machine and lace appliqué design*
- Optional: ¼ yard solid-color cotton twill for embroidery appliqués

- Serger
- Stippling/free-motion/darning foot
- Basic sewing supplies and equipment
* Husqvarna Viking Designer SE LE sewing machine and embroidery design #166 Vintage Lace by Isolde Staab was used for model project.

Purchased lace appliqués may be substituted.

Project notes
Fabric amount listed is for one bib.

Use leftover fabric scraps for diaper bag handle and flowers on bib.

Cutting
From two fat quarters for diaper bag front and back:
- Cut one 21 x 17-inch rectangle from each.

From two fat quarters for diaper bag pockets:
- Cut one 21¼ x 13-inch rectangle from one fat quarter for front pocket.

- Cut one 21¼ x 11½-inch rectangle from second fat quarter for back pocket.

From two fat quarters for diaper bag lining:
- Cut one 21 x 17-inch rectangle from each.

From leftover fat quarter scraps:
- Cut 12 (4 x 3-inch) pieces for handle.
- Cut one 3 x 42-inch strip *or* two 3 x 21¼-inch strips for handle backing.
- Cut one 9 x 18-inch piece for inner base cover.
- Cut one 8 x 10-inch piece for bib flowers.

From quilt batting:
- Cut two 22 x 18-inch rectangles for diaper bag front and back.
- Cut one 3½ x 42-inch strip for diaper bag handle.
- Cut one 8 x 10-inch piece for bib flowers.

From fusible tricot interfacing:
- Cut one 11½ x 21-inch and one 13 x 21-inch rectangles.

Bag Front & Back

Use ½-inch seam allowance unless otherwise stated. Sew with right sides together. Press seams as you sew.

1. Spray-baste wrong side of bag front and back to each piece of batting for bag front and back. Using stippling, free-motion or decorative stitches, quilt as desired.

2. Fuse tricot interfacing rectangles to wrong side of each diaper bag pocket rectangle. Fold both pockets in half with wrong sides together. Press. For front pocket, cut ends at an angle, then turn raw edges to inside and press; topstitch angled ends.

3. Mark vertical center of each pocket; then mark a vertical line 3½ inches on each side of center mark to make three sections each approximately 7 inches (Figure 1).

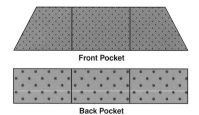

Front Pocket

Back Pocket

Figure 1

4. Place back pocket across bag back 2½ inches from bottom edge (Figure 2); pin in place. Layer lengths of 1½- and ¾-inch-wide ribbon over each section line on pocket and stitch in place through all layers, turning ends under at top.

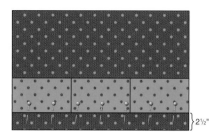

Figure 2

5. Cut two 10-inch lengths of ¾-inch-wide ribbon. Sew center of each length across top of layered ribbons; tie each ribbon in a bow.

6. Trim clear plastic to fit middle pocket section on back pocket and slide under ribbon edges. Straight-stitch over ribbon edges to secure plastic. Slip photo between plastic and pocket.

7. Attach a length of 2-inch-wide ribbon across bottom edge of pocket, stitching across both edges of ribbon. *Note: Bottom edge of ribbon should be just below bottom edge of pocket.*

8. Repeat steps 4, 5 and 7 for bag front.

9. Following manufacturer's instructions, hoop cotton twill and fusible stabilizer; embroider six lace appliqués. *Note: If desired, purchased appliqués may be substituted.* Machine-stitch three appliqués evenly spaced across top of bag on front and back.

Bag & Lining

1. Referring to Figure 3, cut a 2½ x 2½-inch square from the bottom corner of bag front and back.

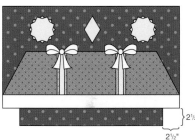

Figure 3

2. With right sides of front and back together, serge or sew side and bottom seams (Figure 4).

Figure 4

3. Fold bag, matching side seams and bottom seam, and stitch across to box the bottom (Figure 5).

Figure 5

4. Repeat steps 1–3 for lining, leaving a 6-inch opening in bottom seam for turning.

5. Place right side of lining over right side of bag.

Handle

1. With right sides together, sew short edges of 4 x 3-inch pieces for handle together. Press seams.

2. Spray-baste joined pieces, quilt batting strip and backing strip together. Machine-quilt using desired method. Trim edges even.

3. Finish edges using 3- or 4-thread serge.

4. Insert handle ends between outside and lining at side seams. Serge or sew around top edge of bag to attach lining to bag, catching ends of handle in stitching. Turn lining through 6-inch opening in bottom seam. Stitch lining seam closed.

5. Cut two 12-inch lengths of ¼-inch-wide ribbon. Fold under one end and position over seam line at center front and back of bag. Topstitch around top edge of bag, catching folded edge of ribbon in stitching. Tie ribbon ends to close bag.

6. Stitch firm interfacing together for inner base. Fold 9 x 18-inch inner base cover in half over base; fold in unfinished edges and press. Topstitch edges. Insert base in bottom of diaper bag.

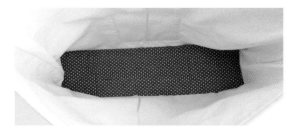

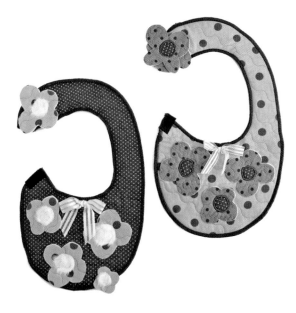

Bib

Note: Bibs should not be left on a child unattended.

1. Spray-baste together fat quarter for bib front and batting. Quilt as desired.

2. Enlarge bib template (page 35) as indicated. Cut bib from quilted fat quarter.

3. Spray-baste together 8 x 10-inch fabric piece and 8 x 10-inch batting piece for bib flowers. Quilt as desired. Using templates provided, cut five flowers from quilted fabric.

4. Position flowers on bib front. Cut flower centers from craft fur. Sew centers onto flowers through bib using a satin stitch.

5. Spray-baste wrong side of bib-lining fat quarter to batting side of bib and trim edges even. Finish edges using a wide 3-thread serge.

6. Straight-stitch hook-and-loop tape in place at neckline closure.

7. Cut a 12-inch length of ⅞-inch-wide ribbon and tie into a bow; trim ends as desired. Straight-stitch through knot to attach bow to bib. ⊗

Sewing Tip

Cut craft fur from the wrong side using the tips of the scissors, being careful not to cut through the fur.

Dots, Flowers & Bows
Flower Templates
Enlarge 200%

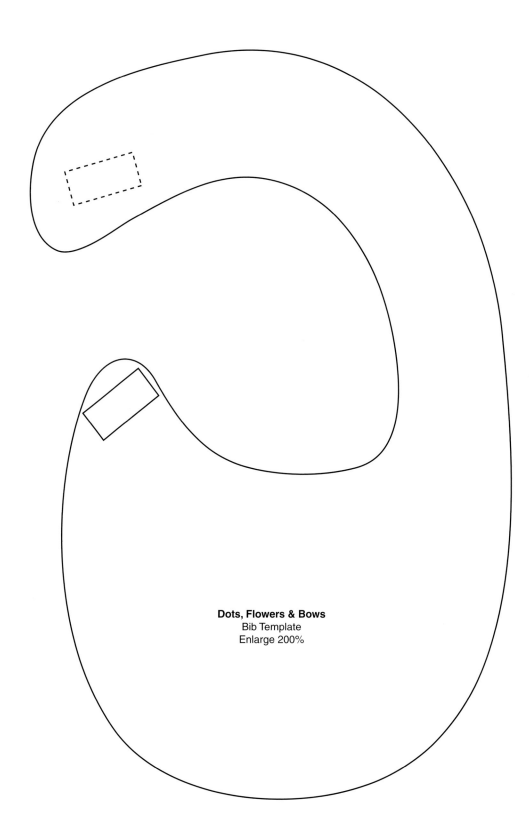

Dots, Flowers & Bows
Bib Template
Enlarge 200%

Color My World

Designs by Carolyn Vagts

*Create a colorful apron and coloring-book tote
in bright colors for a special budding artist.
This is sure to please both mother and child.*

Finished sizes
Apron: Toddler size
Coloring-Book Tote: Approximately 9 x 11 inches,
excluding handles
ID Tag: 6 x 5 inches

Materials
• Cotton fat quarters:
    2 fish print
    2 coordinating print
    2 blue batik
    1 yellow batik
• Scrap green batik for appliqué
• 24 x 22 inches batting
• 10 x 8 inches stiff interfacing
• 4 (1¼-inch) decorative buttons
• Pearl cotton for sewing on buttons
• 10 inches decorative cord for attaching ID tag
• Metal eyelet and eyelet-setting tool
• Paper-backed fusible web
• Fabric paint:
    black
    white
• Basic sewing supplies and equipment

Apron

Cutting
Enlarge and trace apron template (page 40)
as indicated.

From fish print fat quarter:
• Cut one apron on fold.

From blue batik fat quarters:
• Cut one apron on fold.

• Cut four 2½ x 20-inch strips for ties.

Assembly
Use ¼-inch seam allowance (included in
templates). Sew right sides together, unless
otherwise stated. Press seams as you sew.

1. Sew apron pieces, right sides together, as shown
in Figure 1. Turn right side out; press.

Figure 1

2. Fold bottom of apron on fold line to make crayon pockets. Sew across ends. Press. Make a vertical stitch across pocket at center and every 1⅝ inches apart across to make eight individual pockets.

3. Sew 2½-inch-wide strips together on the bias to make one long strip for ties. Press in half lengthwise, wrong sides together. Open and press raw edges to center crease; refold. Cut strip in half. Referring to Figure 2, pin ties to apron. Beginning at one end of tie, topstitch folded edge closed, continuing to opposite end and catching apron in stitching. Knot ends of ties.

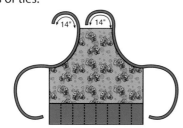

Figure 2

Coloring-Book Tote & ID Tag

Cutting
Cut an 18 x 22-inch piece of batting; layer between one fish print and one coordinating print fat quarter. Quilt as desired.

From quilted fat quarters:
- Cut two 10½ x 14-inch rectangles for tote front and back.

From coordinating print fat quarters:
- Cut two 2½ x 22-inch strips for handles.

From blue batik fat quarters:
- Cut one 13 x 9-inch rectangle for pocket.

From yellow batik fat quarter:
- Cut two 2½ x 22-inch strips for binding.

For fish appliqué:
- Trace appliqué templates (page 39) onto paper side of fusible web to make one fish body, two stripes, one eye, one side fin, one upper fin, one lower fin, one center tail fin, and upper and lower tail fins. Cut out just outside traced lines. Fuse onto fabric as indicated below; cut out on traced lines.

Yellow batik—fish body, and upper and lower tail fins.

Blue batik—side fin and eye.

Green batik—stripes, upper fin, lower fin and center tail fin.

From remaining batting:
• Cut two 1¼ x 22-inch strips for handles.

Assembly

Use ¼-inch seam allowance. Sew right sides together, unless otherwise stated. Press as you sew.

1. Fold pocket rectangle in half with right sides together. Sew raw edges together, leaving an opening for turning (Figure 3). Turn right side out. Press.

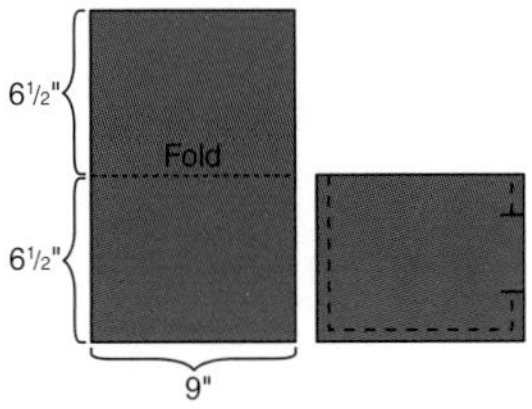

6½"

Fold

6½"

9"

Figure 3

2. Fuse fish appliqué pieces onto pocket. Straight-stitch close to edges of all appliqué pieces except fish body. On fish body, straight-stitch just around edges of mouth only; satin-stitch around edge of body. Paint upper portion of eye black and add small white dots for highlight. Let dry.

3. On tote front, center pocket widthwise and position 1¾ inches from bottom; pin in place (Figure 4). Topstitch pocket to tote front across sides and bottom of pocket.

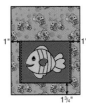

1"   1"

1¾"

Figure 4

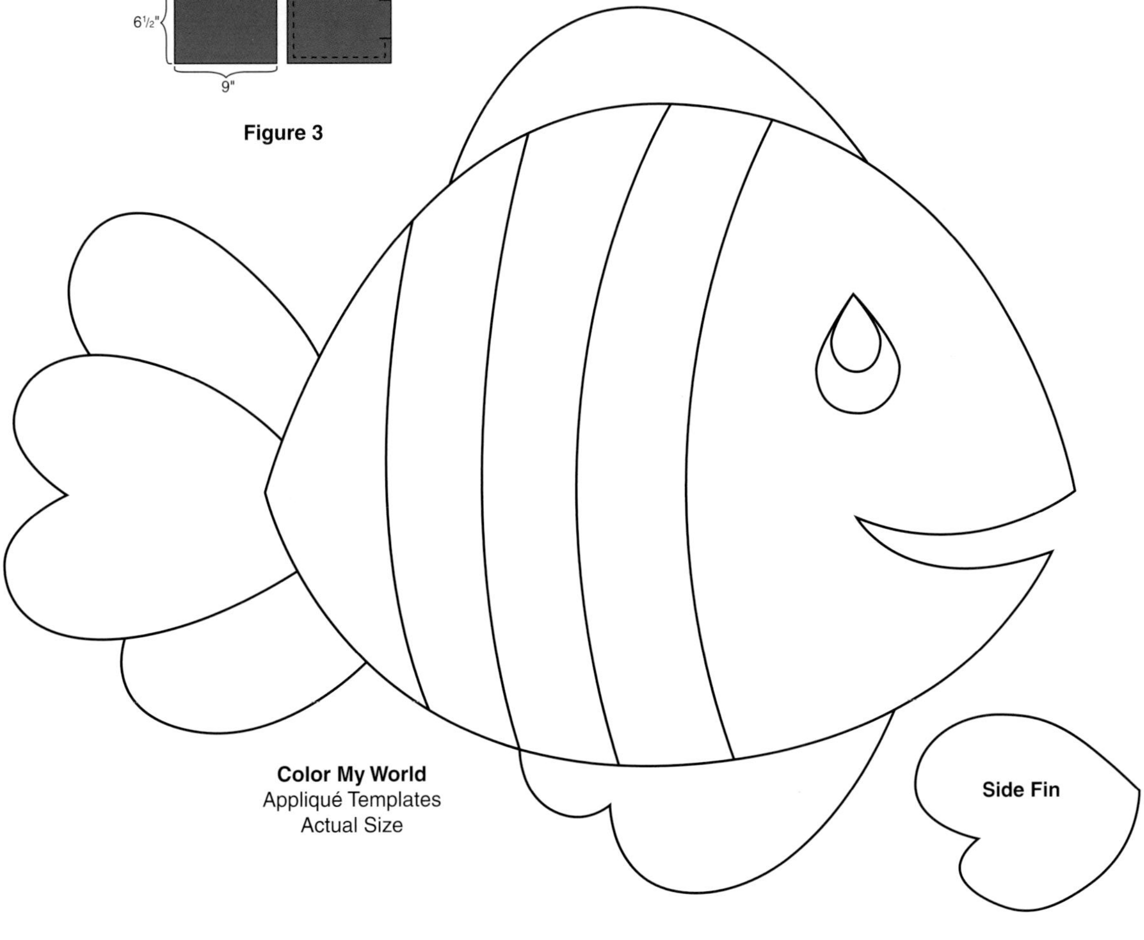

Color My World
Appliqué Templates
Actual Size

Side Fin

Place on Fold

Crayon Apron

Fold Line

Color My World
Template
Enlarge 200%

4. Sew tote front and back together across side and bottom edges. Fold bottom of tote so bottom seam matches side seams. Stitch across bottom seam 1 inch from point at each end to box the bottom (Figure 5). Trim seams. Turn tote right side out.

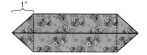

Figure 5

5. Sew binding strips together on the bias to make one long strip. Press strip in half lengthwise with wrong sides together. Sew to top outside edge of tote with raw edges even, turning ends under. Fold binding to inside and hand-stitch in place.

6. Press handle strips in half lengthwise with right sides together. Layer batting on top. Stitch along raw edge, catching batting in the seam. Turn strips right side out. Press. Topstitch down each side of each strip to make handles.

7. Position ends of handles to top front and back of tote, 2 inches from each side and 2 inches from top edge. Turn under raw edges ¼ inch and tack in place across bottom and again 1 inch from first stitching. Sew decorative buttons over handle ends using pearl cotton.

8. For ID tag, trace and fuse fish appliqué pieces onto fusible web as for pocket, but do not cut out mouth on fish. Remove paper backing and fuse pieces onto stiff interfacing. Cut interfacing to fit. Straight-stitch edges of eye, side fin, stripes and center tail fin.

9. Fuse another piece of fabric to the back of the interfacing. Satin-stitch edges. Paint eye as for pocket appliqué. Insert eyelet in top fin and attach tag to handle of tote with cord. Write name on back of tag. ⊗

Source: Fabric from Hoffman California Fabrics.

Yo-Yo Puppy

Design by Carol Zentgraf

Start with a purchased stuffed animal pattern and substitute colorful yo-yos for the legs. They're fun and easy to make with a clever yo-yo maker.

Finished size
Approximately 10 inches tall, sitting

Materials
- Purchased pattern for 10-inch-tall stuffed puppy or other animal
- 8 fat quarters
- Safety eyes and nose as indicated on pattern
- Yo-yo maker for medium yo-yos
- Polyester fiberfill
- Waxed button thread
- 6-inch-long sharp decorator needle
- Permanent fabric adhesive
- Basic sewing supplies and equipment

Cutting
- Follow pattern guide sheet to cut out animal pieces from one fat quarter, eliminating all four legs.

- Cut a 4-inch-wide strip across the width of one fat quarter for collar.

- Cut a 3-inch-wide strip across the width of one fat quarter for collar.

- Follow yo-yo maker instructions to cut out 44 circles for yo-yos from all eight fat quarters.

Assembly

Use ¼-inch seam allowance, unless otherwise stated. Press as you sew.

1. Follow pattern instructions to make and stuff head and body, attaching eyes, nose and ears. Mark placement of legs on body. Make yo-yos from circles following yo-yo maker instructions. Set yo-yos aside.

2. Fold each strip for collar in half lengthwise with right sides together and sew long edges together. Turn right side out and press. Turn short raw edges under and slipstitch ends of each strip together to make a circle. Sew a gathering stitch close to the seamed edge of each strip and pull threads to slightly gather strips. Place ruffles around puppy's neck and pull threads to gather each ruffle securely. Knot thread ends. Tack ruffle edges to neck with a small amount of fabric adhesive.

3. For forelegs, cut a long length of waxed button thread and thread one end through the eye of the decorator needle. Stitching through the openings of the yo-yos, thread 10 yo-yos onto the needle, alternating colors. Pull yo-yos onto the thread, and then stitch back through the yo-yos ⅛ inch from the first stitching.

4. Stitch through the body at one foreleg mark and tie the thread ends together, pulling string of yo-yos close to the body. Apply fabric adhesive to the knot to secure and lightly glue center of first yo-yo to body. Repeat for opposite foreleg.

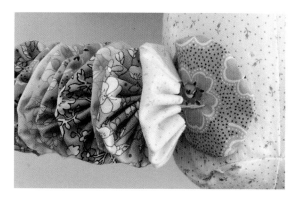

5. Make hind legs in the same manner, using 12 yo-yos for each. ⊗

Sources: Little Darlings 1930s reproduction fabric from Robert Kaufman Fabrics; polyester fiberfill from Fairfield Processing; Fabri-Tac permanent fabric adhesive from Beacon Adhesives.

Down on the Farm Gift Set

Designs by Lorine Mason

Funky farm animals dance across this fun diaper backpack filled with a quilted changing pad and baby-wipe cover.

Finished sizes
Changing Pad: 22½ x 22½ inches
Backpack: 15 x 14½ x 2¼ inches
Baby-Wipes Cover: Varies

Materials
• Fat quarters cotton fabric:
    2 multicolored large prints
    2 blue medium prints
    3 green prints
    2 blue small prints
    3 yellow prints
• 23½ x 23½-inch square fusible fleece
• 2 yards ⅜-inch-wide woven braid or trim
• Buttons:
    decorative (for pocket)
    6 (⅝-inch)
    ⅜-inch
    ½-inch
• Travel-size package of baby wipes
• Basic sewing supplies and equipment

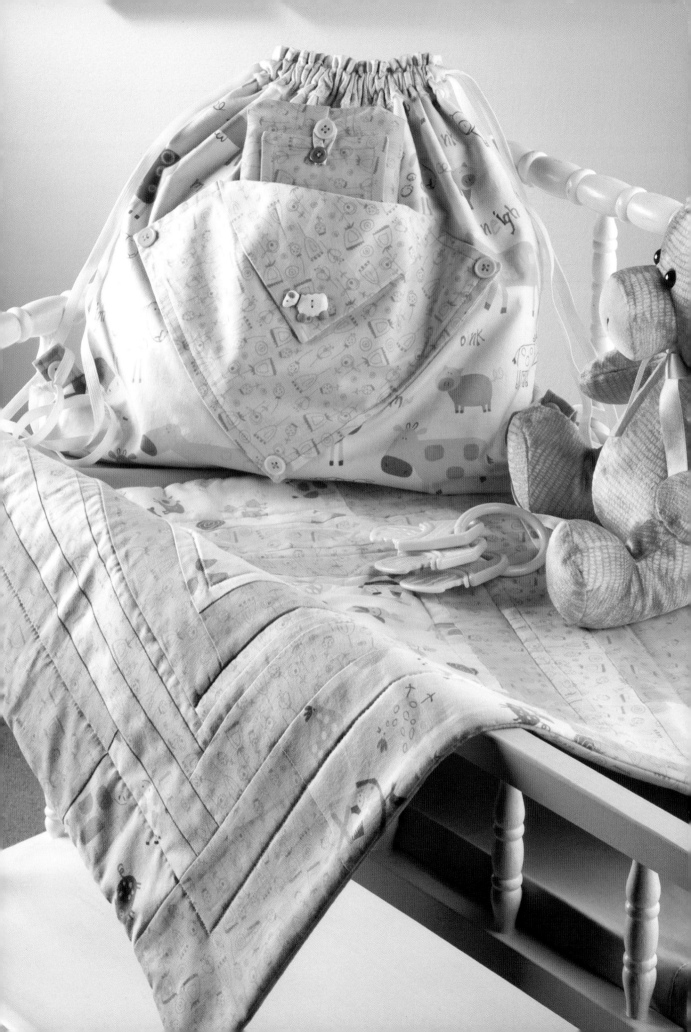

Changing Pad

Cutting

From multicolored large print fat quarters:
• Cut one 18 x 18-inch square (M).

From blue medium print fat quarters:
• Cut one 8¾ x 8¾-inch square (A).

• Cut four 4 x 4¼-inch rectangles (I).

• Cut two 8 x 4¼-inch rectangles (L).

From green print fat quarters:
• Cut two 1-inch strips the width of the fabric (D).

• Cut one 1½-inch strip the width of the fabric (H).

• Cut one 2-inch strip the width of the fabric (F).

From blue small print fat quarters:
• Cut two 1-inch strips the width of the fabric (C).

• Cut one 1½-inch strip the width of the fabric (E).

• Cut two 2-inch strips the width of the fabric (G).

From yellow print fat quarters:
• Cut three 2-inch strips the width of the fabric (B).

• Cut four 8¼ x 4¼-inch rectangles (K).

• Cut two 8½ x 4¼-inch rectangles (J).

• Cut two 18 x 3¼-inch strips (N).

• Cut four 11¾ x 3¼-inch strips (O).

Assembly

Use ¼-inch seam allowance unless otherwise stated. Sew right sides together. Press seams as you sew.

1. Referring to Changing Pad Front Assembly Diagram, assemble pieces A through H as shown, beginning with square A and working in a clockwise direction. ***Notes:*** *Trim each strip to length as it is sewn into place. Reserve a 4-inch length of 1-inch-wide blue small print strip for use in baby-wipes cover.* Sew two I pieces to each J piece and sew to each side of pieced front. Sew two K pieces to each L piece and sew across top and bottom to complete the front.

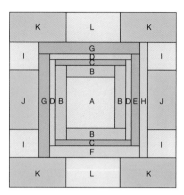

Down on the Farm Gift Set
Changing Pad Front
Assembly Diagram

2. For back of changing pad, sew N strips to opposite sides of the M square. Sew short edges of two O pieces together. Repeat with remaining two O pieces. Sew joined strips across top and bottom of back unit as shown in Changing Pad Back Assembly Diagram.

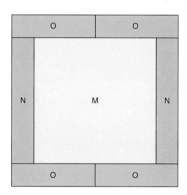

Down on the Farm Gift Set
Changing Pad Back
Assembly Diagram

3. Using a rotary cutter, trim ¼-inch from all sides of pad front, forming a square. Fuse the square of fleece to the wrong side of the pad back. With right sides together, center pad front on top of the back and pin together. Stitch together using a ½-inch seam allowance, leaving a 3-inch opening on one side.

4. Turn right side out. Press. Hand-stitch opening closed. Quilt as desired.

Backpack

Cutting

From multicolored large print:
• Cut one 18 x 18-inch square for backpack front.

From blue medium print:
• Cut one 2 x 6-inch strip for tabs.

From green print:
• Cut two 18 x 18-inch squares for lining front and back.

From blue small print:
• Cut two 10 x 10-inch squares for front pocket.

From yellow print:
• Cut one 18 x 18-inch square for backpack back.

Assembly

Use ½-inch seam allowance. Sew right sides together. Press seams as you sew.

1. Fold tab strip in half lengthwise, right sides together, and stitch along the 6-inch length. Turn right side out and topstitch along each edge. Cut in half and fold to form two tabs. Pin ends together.

2. Pin each tab to backpack front 2 inches from bottom, along sides, with raw edges even. Sew front and back together along side and bottom edges, catching ends of tabs in stitching. Flatten bottom of bag, matching bottom seam to side seams on each side. Sew across bottom 1 inch from point on each side to box bottom. Trim seam allowance. Turn bag right side out.

3. Stitch lining front and back along side and bottom edges. Box bottom of lining in same manner as for bag. Slip lining inside bag, wrong sides together, matching seams and top edges. Pin. Fold top edge 1¾ inches to the front of the bag and press well. Pin. Topstitch through all layers of fabric ¼ inch from the folded edge and again 1 inch from the first stitching to form a casing for the drawstrings.

4. Sew front pocket squares with right sides together, leaving a 2-inch opening on one side. Turn right side out and press. Fold over one corner to form a flap and press well. Center pocket on the front of the bag and pin in place. Stitch along sides and bottom edges of pocket through all layers of fabric.

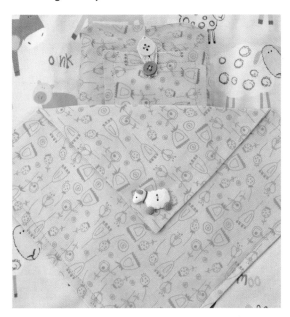

5. Remove stitching in casing side seams from the first two layers of fabric only. Cut braid into 1-yard lengths. Thread one length of braid through from one side, bringing both ends out on opposite side. Thread the second length through from the opposite side to make draw strings. Tie each end through the tab on each side and knot.

6. Sew a decorative button to the pocket flap. Sew a ⅝-inch button to each corner of the pocket and to each tab.

Baby-Wipes Cover

Instructions

1. Measure the length and width of the package of baby wipes. Add 1 inch to the length and 2 inches to the width. Cut a piece of yellow print fabric this length and width for cover bottom.

2. Cut a second piece of yellow print the same length as the cover bottom, but 2 inches wider. Fold in half, matching long edges, and cut down the center for cover top pieces. Turn over and press in 1 inch on one long edge of each piece. Double topstitch close to the raw edge. Pin top cover pieces to bottom cover, right sides together, across the top and bottom edges. Set aside.

3. Using the same length measurement as cover bottom and a 4-inch width, cut one piece of yellow print and one piece of medium blue print fabric for the flap. Sew pieces with right sides together using a ¼-inch seam allowance, leaving the top edge open. Turn right side out and press. Topstitch ¼ inch away from stitched edges.

4. Remove the pins from the cover top/bottom and insert flap with underside of flap against the right side of the cover top. Pin. Stitch around edges of cover using a ½-inch seam allowance. Clip corners. Turn right side out. Press.

5. Fold reserved 4-inch-long blue small print strip in half lengthwise (from Step 1 of Changing Pad Assembly), matching long edges. Sew long edges together using a ¼-inch seam allowance. Turn right side out. Press. Fold strip in half to form a loop. Attach ends of loop to center bottom of flap by sewing ⅜-inch button through them. Sew ⅝-inch button to cover top to correspond with loop. *Note: Sew button to both halves of opening.*

6. Insert baby wipes in cover. Draw loop over button to close flap. ⊗

Source: Fabric from Robert Kaufman Fabrics.

Sewing Tip

Use sticky notes or labels to mark fabric with dimensions as you cut for easy identification.

Comforts of Home

As family and friends travel far from home, a special quilt or pillow makes a great gift to remind them of loved ones back home. These simple-to-sew quilts are designed in a variety of sizes for every faraway need: lap-sized for aging parents; twin-bed-sized for college students; and for the space challenged, comforting home memories stitched up as a pretty pillow set.

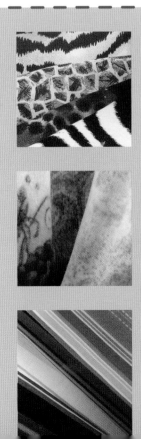

Windmill Twin Quilt

Design by Carol Zentgraf

Pieced quilts are a great way to showcase the coordinating prints in a favorite fabric collection.

Finished size
75½ x 100½ inches

Materials
• Fat quarters for quilt front:
    3 each of 11 prints
    2 each of 2 prints
• 44/45-inch-wide striped fabric:
    1½ yards each of 4 top prints for back
    ¾ yard of one top print for binding
• 82 x 107 inches batting
• Bias-tape maker
• Basic sewing supplies and equipment

Cutting
From quilt front print fat quarters:
Note: Cut 192 squares total.

• Cut 16 (8 x 8-inch) squares from each of 11 prints for a total of 176 squares.

• Cut 8 (8 x 8-inch) squares from each of 2 prints for a total of 16 squares.

• Subcut each 8 x 8-inch square in half diagonally and stack triangles according to fabric print.

From fabric for back:
• Cut one 40 x 53-inch rectangle from each print for back.

From fabric for binding:
• Cut 9½ yards of 1⅞-inch-wide bias for binding.

Assembly
Use ¼-inch seam allowance. Sew right sides together, unless otherwise stated. Press seams as you sew.

1. Plan fabric placement for each windmill block, choosing two contrasting colors for each block. To assemble each block, sew contrasting triangles together in pairs along the long edges. Trim the block to 7 x 7 inches. Sew four blocks together to create the windmill design (Figure 1). Press. Trim windmill block to 13 x 13 inches. Repeat to assemble a total of 48 windmill blocks.

Figure 1

2. Arrange windmill blocks in eight horizontal rows of six blocks each. Sew blocks in each row together. Press seam allowances to one side, alternating direction on adjacent rows.

3. Sew the rows together, matching the corners of the squares. Press.

4. Sew long edges of two back rectangles together and press seams. Repeat with remaining two back rectangles. Sew joined rectangles together, matching seams, to make a 79½ x 104½-inch quilt back.

5. Cut batting to fit quilt back. Sandwich batting between back and front. Beginning in the center and working toward the outside, pin layers together along seam lines and outer edges of the top. Stitch in the ditch along block seams to quilt. Trim batting and back even with edges of top.

6. Sew bias strips together. Trim seam allowances to ⅛ inch and press to one side. Follow bias-tape maker instructions to press strips into bias tape.

7. Open tape. On front of quilt, with raw edges even, sew narrow side of bias tape around edges, mitering corners.

8. Fold tape to back of quilt and pin in place. Stitch in the ditch on the front of the quilt, catching the edges of the binding on the back of the quilt to secure. ⊗

Sources: Fabric from Michael Miller Fabrics; bamboo batting from Fairfield Processing; bias-tape maker from Clover Needlecraft Inc.

It's Popping Up Pillows!

Designs by Carol Zentgraf

Create simple, fast and inexpensive gifts when you combine scraps of your favorite fat quarters to make these mix-and-match pieced pillows.

Square Pillow

Finished size
18 x 18 inches

Materials
• Fat quarters:
  2 large print
  1 each 2 coordinating prints
• 18 x 18-inch pillow form
• Basic sewing supplies and equipment

Cutting
From large print fat quarters:
  • Cut four 10 x 10-inch squares.

From each of coordinating print fat quarter:
  • Cut two 10 x 10-inch squares.

Assembly
Use ½-inch seam allowance. Sew right sides together. Press as you sew.

1. Sew each large-print square to a coordinating-print square to make four two-square units.

2. Sew two units together, alternating large-print squares, to make pillow front. Repeat to make pillow back.

3. Sew pillow front and back together, leaving a 10-inch opening in center of one side for turning. Turn right side out. Press, turning under opening seam allowance.

4. Insert pillow form. Slipstitch opening closed.

Rectangular Pillow

Finished size
12 x 16 inches

Materials
• Fat quarters:
    2 large print
    1 each 2 coordinating prints
• 12 x 16-inch pillow form
• Basic sewing supplies and equipment

Cutting

From large print fat quarter:
• Cut one 13 x 9-inch rectangle for center front panel.

• Cut one 13 x 17-inch rectangle for back.

From one coordinating print fat quarter:
• Cut two 2 x 13-inch strips for contrast borders.

From second coordinating print fat quarter:
• Cut two 4 x 13-inch strips for end panels.

Assembly
Use ½-inch seam allowance. Sew with right sides together, unless otherwise stated. Press seams as you sew.

1. Sew a contrast border to each side of center front panel. Sew an end panel to each contrast border to make pillow front. Press seam allowances open.

2. Sew pillow front to back, leaving a 10-inch opening in center of lower edge for turning; turn right side out. Press, turning under opening seam allowance.

3. Insert pillow form and slipstitch opening closed. ⊗

Sources: Fabric from Michael Miller Fabrics; Home Elegance pillow forms from Fairfield Processing.

A Day at the Zoo Quilt

Design by Linda Turner Griepentrog

After an action-packed day at the zoo, it's likely your little one will need a well-deserved nap, and this button-quilted animal throw is the perfect coverup.

Finished size
40½ x 48½ inches

Materials
• 9 or more animal-print fat quarters
• 44/45-inch-wide fabric:
    ½ yard animal print for borders
    1½ yard animal print for backing
• 45 x 53 inches lightweight batting
• 30 animal buttons
• Basic sewing supplies and equipment

Cutting
From fat quarters:
 • Cut a total of 20 (8½ x 8½-inch) squares
   for blocks.

 • Cut random-length strips 2½ inches wide
   to total 5⅓ yards when joined for binding.

From fabric for borders:
 • Cut four 4½-inch-wide strips the width
   of the fabric.

Assembly
Use ¼-inch seam allowance. Sew right sides together, unless otherwise stated. Press seams as you sew.

1. Arrange blocks as desired in five vertical rows of four blocks each. Sew blocks together in each row, pressing seam allowances in alternating directions on adjacent rows.

2. Join rows to form quilt center, matching block seams (Figure 1). Press seam allowances in one direction.

Figure 1

3. Add a border strip to each side of the pieced center, and then to the ends (Figure 2). Press seam allowances toward borders.

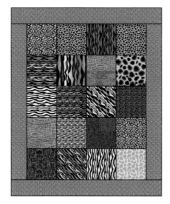

Figure 2

4. Place quilt backing fabric wrong side up. Lightly spray with temporary adhesive. Adhere batting. Lightly spray batting with temporary adhesive and adhere quilt top right side up. Smooth in place to eliminate wrinkles.

5. Sew binding strips end to end and press seams open. Fold in in half lengthwise, wrong sides together and press to make 1¼-inch-wide binding. With right sides together, matching raw edges, sew binding to the quilt, mitering corners. Turn binding to the back of the quilt and hand-stitch in place.

6. Sew animal buttons at block junctions to hold layers together. To avoid knots on underside of the quilt, anchor threads under the button on the quilt right side. ⊗

Sources: Wildlife and Great Outdoor animal button collections from JHB International Inc.; Warm & White batting from The Warm Company, thread from Sulky of America.

Make a Label

To commemorate a special trip to the zoo, create a label for the quilt back by printing it on the computer. Open a document, insert a photo and have your child tell a story about the adventure. Print the label on a pretreated fabric sheet following the manufacturer's instructions. Trim to size, turn under the edges and fuse to the quilt backing using ¼-inch-wide fusible web tape around the edges.

May 10,

Grandma took Alli and me to the zoo

Scrappy Rag Quilt

Design by Lucy Fazely

Try this quilt-as-you-sew technique to make quilts quickly and easily. This method works well with other fabrics too. Just be sure to sew the scrappy quilt blocks with a large seam allowance.

Finished size

Quilt: 64 x 80 inches

Materials

- Flannel fat quarters:
    20 light
    20 dark
- 20 (8 x 16-inch) pieces batting
- ⅔ yard 44/45-inch-wide flannel fabric for binding
- Muliticolored machine-quilting thread
- Basic sewing supplies and equipment

Cutting

From flannel fat quarters:
- Cut each fat quarter into two 10 x 18-inch pieces.

From fabric for binding:
- Cut eight 2½ x 44-inch strips.

Assembly

Use 1-inch seam allowance. Press seams as you sew.

1. Layer one 10 x 18-inch flannel piece facedown, center a 8 x 16-inch piece of batting next, followed by the matching flannel piece, faceup. Spray-baste layers together. Stitch a large X from corner to corner (Figure 1). Repeat to make a total of 40 units.

Figure 1

2. Sew one light unit and one dark unit together along one long side to make a total of 20 blocks (Figure 2).

Figure 2

3. Referring to the Assembly Diagram, arrange blocks in five vertical rows of four blocks each. Sides of blocks with raw edges exposed will be the front side of quilt. With back sides together, sew blocks together to form rows; join rows to form the quilt.

This is a very forgiving quilt, so cutting and piecing do not have to be exact.

Use a variegated thread that matches the color theme of the quilt for added interest.

Scrappy Rag Quilt
Assembly Diagram

4. Trim 1 inch from the outer edges. Sew binding strips together to make one long strip. Fold wrong sides together along length, matching long edges, and press. Sew binding on right side of quilt, matching raw edges with outer raw edges of quilt. Fold binding over edge of quilt and hand-stitch in place on back of quilt.

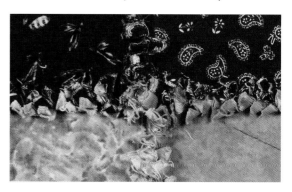

5. Clip block seam allowances ¾ inch deep and approximately ½ inch apart. Wash and dry quilt several times for best rag effect. *Note: Use a commercial machine to launder the first few times, as threads can clog an ordinary washing machine.* ⊗

Sources: Warm & Natural cotton batting from The Warm Company; Star Multicolored Quilting and Craft Thread from Coats & Clark.

Warm & Cozy Flannel Throw

Design by Chris Malone

Quilt a pretty and pratical flannel fat quarter quilt to keep your friends and family warm on cool winter nights.

Finished size
39 x 39 inches

Materials
• Quality quilter's flannel:
    9 coordinating fat quarters for front
    2½ yards of 44/45-inch-wide for backing
• 49 (5¼ x 5¼-inch) squares batting
• Soluble fabric glue stick
• Freezer paper
• Optional: walking foot
• Basic sewing supplies and equipment

Pattern notes
Prewash, dry and iron flannel. Preshrink batting if using cotton.

To use freezer paper as a cutting or sewing guide, draw the circle pattern onto the dull side of the paper and cut out. To use, press the shiny side onto fabric for about 3 seconds. Paper will hold while cutting or sewing, then can be peeled off and reused about 5 times.

Cutting
From fat quarters:
• Cut a total of 49 (6½ x 6½-inch) squares for blocks.

• Cut 10 (4-inch) circles from freezer paper and use to cut 25 circles.

From flannel for backing:
• Cut 49 (6½ x 6½-inch) squares for backing blocks.

• Cut 10 (4-inch) circles from freezer paper and use to cut 25 circles.

Assembly
Use ½-inch seam allowance. Press seams as you sew.

1. Arrange blocks in seven rows of seven blocks for the face of the quilt. Layer each fat-quarter circle with a flannel backing circle, both with right sides up.

2. Referring to the Assembly Diagram, place layered circles in centers of alternating blocks.

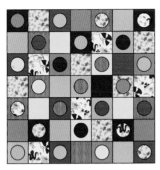

Warm & Cozy Flannel Throw
Assembly Diagram

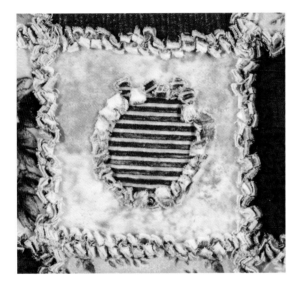

3. Center a batting square on the wrong side of each backing block and adhere in place with a small amount of fabric glue stick.

4. Cut 10 (3-inch circles) from freezer paper. Keeping the arranged order of rows, iron a circle of freezer paper to the center of either the circle or the plain block. Pin this block to the layered backing block with wrong sides together. Sew around the edge of the circle using matching or contrasting thread. Peel off circle and repeat to complete all blocks in this manner.

5. Clip the seam allowance on each circle appliqué by making snips ¼–⅜ inch apart perpendicular to the seam line, taking care not to clip into the stitching (Figure 1).

Figure 1

6. To assemble a row, pin blocks with back sides together and sew with a ½-inch seam allowance.

7. Join rows in the same manner, matching seams.

8. Clip each seam, making snips perpendicular to seam line and ¼–⅜ inch apart. To snip corners, make two diagonal cuts as shown in Figure 2.

Figure 2

9. To fray edges, wash throw in commercial washing machine and dry in dryer, checking occasionally for accumulated lint. Shake quilt outside when dry. ⊗

Source: Soft & Bright needle-punched polyester batting from The Warm Company.

Sewing Tip

This project is a good way to use up small batting scraps. Spring-loaded scissors are easier to use for clipping. There is even a pair of scissors marketed especially for this type of raggedy-edge quilt.

Tumbling Stripes Throw

Design by Carol Zentgraf

Stripes are always fun to work with. Sew this fast and fun quilt with the stripes tumbling horizontally and vertically on this colorful throw.

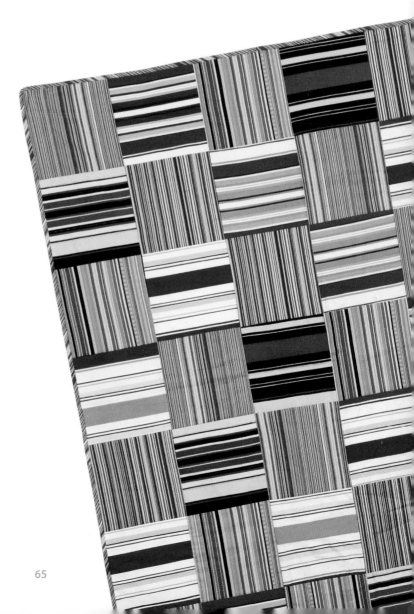

Finished size
57 x 65½ inches

Materials
• Fat quarters:
   2 each of six stripes for front
   12 of one, or combination of stripes
      for back
• ½ yard 44/45-inch-wide striped fabric
   for binding
• 63 x 72 inches batting
• Bias-tape maker
• Basic sewing supplies and equipment

Cutting
From front stripes fat quarters:
 • Cut seven 9 x 9-inch squares from each
   of the six stripes for a total of 42 squares.

From back stripes fat quarters:
 • Cut 12 (18 x 18-inch) squares.

From fabric for binding:
 • Cut 1⅞-inch-wide bias strips to total
   7 yards when joined.

Assembly

Use ¼-inch seam allowance. Sew right sides together, unless otherwise stated. Press seams as you sew.

1. Arrange front squares into seven horizontal rows of six squares each, placing one square of each fabric in each row. Alternate the direction of the stripes for each block and on alternating rows.

2. Sew squares together in each row. Press seam allowances to one side, alternating the direction on adjacent rows.

3. Sew the rows together, matching the corners of the squares. Press.

4. Sew back squares together in four rows of three squares each. Cut batting to fit the back.

5. Sandwich batting between back and front. Beginning in the center and working toward the outside, pin layers together along seam lines and outer edges of the top. Stitch in the ditch along block seams to quilt. Trim batting and back even with edges of top.

6. Sew bias strips together. Trim seam allowances to ⅛ inch and press to one side. Follow bias-tape maker instructions to press strips into bias tape.

7. Open tape. On front of quilt, with raw edges even, sew narrow side of bias tape around edges, mitering corners.

8. Fold tape to back of quilt and pin in place. Stitch in the ditch on the front of the quilt, catching the edges of the binding on the back of the quilt to secure. ⊗

Sources: Fabric from Michael Miller Fabrics; bamboo batting from Fairfield Processing; bias-tape maker from Clover Needlecraft Inc.

Bags & More

You'll have it in the bag when you decide to give a design from this chapter. Whether your need is to say bon voyage to a dear friend, to create a memorable wedding party gift, a gift exchange for your sewing circle, or a custom-designed wine tote for a special dinner engagement, you'll find the perfect bag in this chapter. Who says you can't take it all with you?

In-a-Snap Purse

Design by Janis Bullis

Our roomy quilted bag imitates the style you might see in a designer boutique. A hinged frame and magnetic-snap front closure make this bag a dream to carry. Make it all your own by choosing three coordinating fabric colors and a matching faux suede for the handle.

Finished size
13 x 10½ x 4 inches

Materials
• Cotton fat quarters:
>   3 pink
>   1 teal
>   1 yellow
• ¼ yard teal faux suede or leather
• ¾ yard 20-inch-wide heavyweight nonwoven interfacing
• ¾ yard 20-inch-wide lightweight quilt batting
• ⅓ yard ⅜-inch filler cord
• 8-inch tubular hinged metal purse frame
• 4 (1¼-inch) metal D rings
• 4 (9mm) rivets
• 11 x 4½-inch piece ¼-inch-thick foam-core board
• 1 (1-inch) decorative button
• 1 magnetic snap closure
• Basic sewing supplies and equipment

Cutting

Enlarge templates as indicated below.

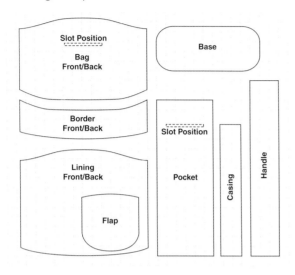

In-a-Snap Purse
Templates
1 square = 1"

From pink fat quarter:
• Cut two bag front/backs.

• Cut one base for lining.

• Cut two casings.

• Cut one pocket.

• Cut two lining front/backs.

From teal fat quarter:
• Cut two border front/backs.

• Cut one base.

From yellow fat quarter:
• Cut two flaps.

From faux suede:
• Cut two handles.

From nonwoven interfacing:
• Cut two lining front/backs.

• Cut one base.

• Cut one flap.

• Cut two 1¼ x 18-inch pieces for handles.

From filler cord:
• Cut two 6-inch lengths.

From quilt batting:
• Cut two lining front/backs.

• Cut one base.

• Cut one flap.

Assembly

Templates include ¼-inch seam allowance. Sew with right sides together. Press as you sew.

1. Staystitch upper inside corners of border just inside seam allowance. Clip seam allowance to staystitching. With right sides together, pin and stitch border to bag front/back at long edge, spreading clipped seam to fit. Press seam open.

2. Measure and mark center of front/back assembly. Draw two lines at 45-degree angles through center mark. Draw parallel lines 2 inches from each line across front/back assembly (Figure 1).

Figure 1

3. Pin and baste quilt batting to wrong side of front/back. Using a slightly longer stitch, quilt through both layers along all marked lines.

4. Baste interfacing to batting side along all edges using a scant ¼-inch seam allowance. Repeat steps 1–4 for remaining border and front/back pieces.

5. Measure and mark center of base. Pin quilt batting to wrong side of base, mark lines and quilt as for front/back assembly (Figure 2); then baste interfacing to batting side along all edges using a scant ¼-inch seam allowance.

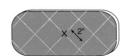

Figure 2

6. Quilt and interface one flap in the same manner, except mark the lines 1 inch apart. With right sides together, pin and stitch the remaining flap piece to quilted/interfaced piece along curved edges (Figure 3). Clip curves. Turn right side out through open straight edge. Press flat. Topstitch curved edges. Do not stitch open edge.

Figure 3

7. Staystitch lower curved edges of front/back assembly just inside seam allowance. Clip to staystitching. With right sides together, pin and stitch base to front/back assembly, spreading clipped seam to fit at curves (Figure 4).

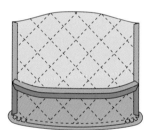

Figure 4

8. Transfer slot position to wrong side of pocket fabric. With right sides facing, pin pocket to bag center front with upper raw edges even. Stitch on transferred lines. Cut through center of slot area and clip corners to create opening (Figure 5). Turn pocket to wrong side of front. Press flat.

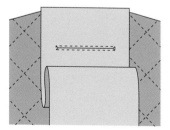

Figure 5

9. Fold lower edge of pocket up. Holding pocket separately from bag, stitch side seams. Baste top edges of pocket to upper edge of front (Figure 6).

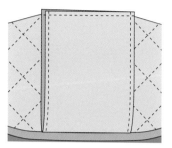

Figure 6

10. Fasten magnetic snap closure to wrong side of flap and to front of bag through pocket side; do not attach closure through both sides of pocket. Baste flap to upper edge of bag over pocket opening.

11. Baste handle interfacing to center of each handle on wrong side. With right sides together, fold handle in half lengthwise and stitch along long edges (Figure 7). Turn to right side and press flat with seam centered. Insert rivets 1½ inches from each end.

Figure 7

12. At center of handle, lay one length of filler cord along seam line and wrap fabric around it. Hand-stitch folds to cover cord. Slip two D rings over handle (Figure 8).

Figure 8

13. With right side of handle facing right side of bag, pin ends (tilted slightly) to top edge of bag at each side of flap (Figure 9). Repeat steps 11–13 for second handle on opposite side of bag.

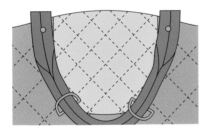

Figure 9

14. With right sides together, sew side seams of lining front/back. Staystitch lower curved edges just inside seam allowance; clip to staystitching (refer to Step 7 and Figure 4). With right sides together, pin and stitch lining front/back to lining base, leaving a 5-inch opening on one edge.

15. With bag right side out and lining wrong side out, pull lining over bag and pin upper raw edges together. Stitch through all layers using a scant ¼-inch seam allowance.

16. Turn under ¼ inch on each short edge of casing; stitch or fuse in place. With wrong sides together, fold each casing in half lengthwise. Pin and stitch to center top inside edges of bag (Figure 10).

Figure 10

17. With right sides facing out, separate bag from lining. Working through opening in lining, slide tubular frames into each casing. Firmly squeeze together opposite ends of frame to align holes. Slide self-piloting metal posts through loops to secure the frame; attach caps. Slipstitch lining closed.

18. Stitch decorative button to flap. Stitch D rings to handles. Trace base template onto foam-core board and cut out. Slip into bottom of bag. ⊗

Source: Tubular purse frame and magnetic snap closure from Ghee's.

A Gift for Her

Design by Sheila Zent

What bride wouldn't love to receive a travel case crafted especially for her jewelry? This handy organizer with three see-through pockets rolls and ties for easy packing.

Finished size
Approximately 15 x 9 inches, open

Materials
• 2 matching cotton fat quarters
• ⅜ yard nonfusible polyester fleece
• ¼ yard mediumweight clear vinyl
• Lightweight fusible interfacing
• 3 (7-inch) zippers
• 1 yard ⅜-inch-wide grosgrain ribbon
• Basic sewing supplies and equipment

Cutting
From fat quarters:
• Cut one 13½ x 10-inch rectangle for organizer backing.

• Cut one 4½ x 10-inch rectangle for bottom pocket backing.

• Cut one 5 x 10-inch rectangle for middle pocket backing.

• Cut one 5½ x 10-inch rectangle for top pocket backing.

• Use template (page 77) to cut two flaps.

• Fuse interfacing to wrong side of fabric. Trace zipper band template (page 77) three times onto interfaced side of fabric. Transfer zipper opening placement lines. Cut out bands, leaving openings uncut for now.

From vinyl:
• Cut one 4½ x 10-inch rectangle for bottom pocket.

• Cut one 5 x 10-inch rectangle for middle pocket.

• Cut one 5½ x 10-inch rectangle for top pocket.

From fleece:
• Cut one 13½ x 10-inch rectangle for organizer backing.

• Cut one 4½ x 10-inch rectangle for bottom pocket.

• Cut one 5 x 10-inch rectangle for middle pocket.

• Cut one 5½ x 10-inch rectangle for top pocket.

• Use template (page 77) to cut two flaps.

Assembly

Use ½-inch seam allowance unless otherwise stated. Press as you sew.

1. Baste organizer backing, flaps and pocket backings to corresponding fleece pieces around outside edges. Set aside.

2. Press under ¼ inch along bottom edge of each zipper band. With right sides together, place the top edge of one band at the top of a vinyl pocket piece, matching raw edges. *Note: Pin in seam allowances only, as pin holes will be permanent in vinyl.* Stitch on traced lines for opening. In center of opening, slit through all layers and cut into corners (Figure 1).

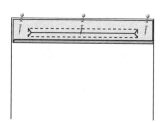

Figure 1

3. Turn the band right side out through the cut opening. Finger-press seams around the opening to crease the vinyl. With fabric side up, press opening neatly. Pin and stitch top raw edges together and opposite folded edge in place through the vinyl. Repeat for each zipper band and vinyl pocket.

4. Center zipper opening over a zipper and topstitch around the opening to hold the zipper in place. With right side up, place the vinyl pocket over the corresponding pocket backing; baste layers together close to the outside edges. Repeat with each vinyl pocket, zipper and pocket backing. Topstitch vertically through bottom pocket to divide into equal sections.

5. With right sides together, stitch top edge of bottom pocket to bottom edge of middle pocket. Trim and grade seam allowances. Push seam allowance down and edgestitch along lower edge of seam to flatten (Figure 2). Attach top edge of middle pocket to lower edge of top pocket in same manner.

Figure 2

Sewing & Pressing Vinyl

Set sewing machine to a medium-long stitch length. A short stitch makes the vinyl susceptible to tearing.

Switch to a Teflon sewing machine foot to keep the vinyl from sticking and dragging while sewing. If a Teflon foot is not available, layer tissue paper or tear-away stabilizer between the vinyl and your regular presser foot. Also, stitch with the vinyl side down and fabric side up.

Avoid pinning as much as possible, choosing only to pin in areas that won't be seen upon completion, such as in the seam allowance or directly along the stitch line.

Set iron on low heat (acetate or polyester setting) without steam. Cover vinyl with a cotton press cloth (washed muslin makes a good press cloth). After pressing, remove press cloth and allow the vinyl to cool before lifting from the pressing surface.

6. Cut ribbon in half. On right side of organizer backing, baste one half at center top edge of backing. Baste remaining half at tip of flap (Figure 3). Sew short edges of flaps together, being careful not to catch ribbon except at tip where it is basted. Trim corner seam allowances and turn right side out. Press. Baste open edges together.

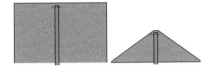

Figure 3

7. With raw edges matching, pin flap to top pocket, centered between seam allowances. Stitch. Place backing over pocket assembly, right sides together, and pin corners. Pin sides, easing backing edges to fit pocket edges. *Note: Back is cut longer than pockets to allow extra fabric for wrapping.* Stitch around outside edges, leaving a 5-inch opening at the top. Clip corner seam allowances and turn right side out through opening. Tuck seam allowances to the inside and slipstitch opening closed. Press using a warm iron. ⊗

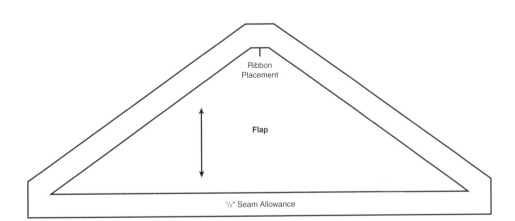

Ribbon
Placement

Flap

½" Seam Allowance

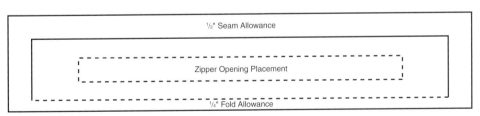

½" Seam Allowance

Zipper Opening Placement

¼" Fold Allowance

Zipper Band

A Gift for Her
Templates
Enlarge 200%

Pretty & Pieced

Designs by Connie Kauffman

These sweet gift bags are easy to make and are a beautiful way to wrap a gift. By varying the placement of fabrics, four bags can be made from the same six fat quarters.

Finished size
Approximately 7¾ x 18½ inches

Materials for Two Bags
• 6 coordinating cotton fat quarters
• 40 inches ¼-inch-wide ribbon
• Basic sewing supplies and equipment

Simple Block Bag Cutting
From one fat quarter:
• Cut one 16½ x 11-inch rectangle for bottom portion of bag.

From one fat quarter:
• Cut one 16½ x 8¾-inch rectangle for top portion of bag.

From each of the remaining four fat quarters:
• Cut two 3¼ x 3¼-inch squares. Cut each square on each diagonal to make four triangles from each square (Figure 1).

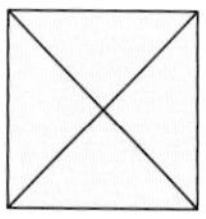

Figure 1

From two of the four fat quarters:
• Cut one 1 x 16½-inch strip from each.

Simple Block Bag Assembly
Use ¼-inch seam allowance unless otherwise stated. Sew right sides together. Press as you sew.

1. Sew four different-color triangles together to make eight blocks, using the same color placement for each block (Figure 2).

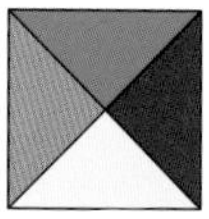

Figure 2

2. Sew the blocks into a row; sew one 1 x 16½-inch strip on each side of the strip on each side of the pieced row to create a border. (Figure 3).

Figure 3

3. Sew border to top and bottom sections (Figure 4).

Figure 4

4. Mark 5½ inches from top edge of bag and sew a small horizontal buttonhole for drawstring; cut open. Press top raw edge under ¼ inch.

5. Fold bag right sides together and sew side and bottom edges. Finish edges with serger or zigzag stitches.

6. Turn top of bag to wrong side 2½–2¾ inches and press. Stitch on inside folded edge and again approximately ¾ inch above that, making sure buttonhole is between the two sewn lines.

7. Turn bag right side out. Press. Cut ribbon in half. Thread one length through buttonhole and pull ends even. *Note: Set remaining length aside for Easy Gift Bag.* At center back of casing, stitch through ribbon to prevent it from pulling out.

Easy Gift Bag Cutting & Assembly

Use two of the six fat quarters for top and bottom sections, and the remaining four fat quarters for pieced section.

Follow instructions for Simple Block Bag, except cut and piece the border as follows:

From two fat quarters:
• Cut one 1 x 16½-inch strip from each.

From one fat quarter:
• Cut six 2 x 2½-inch rectangles.

From one fat quarter:
• Cut five 2 x 2½-inch rectangles.

Assemble rectangles alternately into a row, matching 2-inch sides. Trim excess fabric from row to fit. Sew strips to top and bottom of pieced row to create a border. ⊗

Sewing Tip

To create a fast gift bag, instead of quilting a border, simply cut a 2½ x 16½-strip and edge each side with a 1 x 16½-inch strip of coordinating fabric.

A Stitch in Time Tote

Design by Willow Ann Sirch

Use fat quarters to sew an attractive tote bag that makes a great gift.

Finished size
16½ X 12 X 3½ inches, excluding handles

Materials
• Coordinating cotton fat quarters:
    1 each of 8 prints in gold, orange and red
       (A–C and E–I) for checkerboard squares
       and Roman stripes
    1 white print (J) for triangles
    3 of 1 red print (D) for lining, handles and
       2 diagonal strips
    2 of 1 orange print (K) for outer back,
       bottom and side gussets
• 12½ x 4½ inches iron-on interfacing
• Quilter's square ruler
• Basic sewing supplies and equipment

Cutting
From A and B fat quarters:
• Cut four 1½ x 22-inch strips for checkerboard
  squares from each.

From C and E–H fat quarters:
• Cut two 1½ x 22-inch strips for Roman stripes
  from each.

From D fat quarters:
• Cut two 1½ x 22-inch strips for Roman stripes.

• Cut two 18 x 5-inch strips for handles.

• Cut one 16½ x 4½-inch strip for lining bottom.

• Cut two 12½ x 4½-inch strips for
  lining side gusset.

• Cut one 16½ x 12½-inch rectangle for
  lining front and back.

From I and J fat quarters:
• Cut two 3½ x 22-inch strips for triangle squares.

From K fat quarters:
• Cut one 16½ x 4½-inch strip for tote bottom.

• Cut two 12½ x 4½-inch strips
  for outer side gusset.

• Cut one 16½ x 12½-inch rectangle for
  outer back.

Assembly

Use ¼-inch seam allowance unless otherwise stated. Sew right sides together. Press seams as you sew.

1. Match right sides two A strips short ends together. Sew, press seams to one side. Repeat with remaining two A strips. Join B strips in same manner. Sew A and B strips together alternately along long edges. Press seams in same direction.

2. Cutting across the seams, cut 16 (1½-inch-wide) strips from the A/B unit. Sew four strips together in checkerboard pattern and trim into 4½-inch square (Figure 1). Repeat with remaining strips to make 4 checkerboard squares.

Figure 1

3. Match right sides of each pair of strips C, D, E, F, G and H, short ends together. Sew; press seams to one side. Sew strips together another along one long side in the following order: C, D, E, F, G, H. Press seams in one direction.

4. Using a quilter's square ruler, cut four 4½-inch squares on the diagonal from pieced strips, aligning the middle of each square with the seam that runs through the middle of the 6-stripe pieced square. Press seams in one direction (Figure 2).

Figure 2

5. Match right sides of I strips together on short ends to make two long I strips. Repeat with the J strips. Sew I and J strips together along long edges. Using quilter's square ruler, cut eight triangles with a 6¼-inch base and 4½-inch sides, positioning triangles so they form two half-size triangles that meet along the middle seam. Sew triangles together along the base to make four squares. Press seams in one direction (Figure 3).

Figure 3

6. Following the Assembly Diagram, arrange squares in sewing order. Sew squares together to make pieced front of tote. Press seams in one direction.

A Stitch in Time Tote
Assembly Diagram

7. Center and fuse interfacing to tote bottom strip. With right sides together, sew tote bottom along one side to bottom long side of pieced front. Press seams open. Sew opposite bottom edge to outer back bottom edge. Press seams open. Sew outer side gussets along sides and bottom to make outer tote. Follow same procedure to sew the tote lining.

8. With right sides together, sew lining to outer tote along top edge, leaving a 4-inch opening. Press seams open. Turn right side out through opening. Press lightly.

9. Press under short edges of handles ⅜ inch. Fold long edges to the center, then fold handles in half along length. Topstitch around all edges. Topstitch ends of handles to front and back of tote approximately 6 inches from each side. ⊗

Appliquéd Wine Bag

Design by Chris Malone

A nice bottle of wine is an appreciated gift when family and friends get together. What better way to dress up a bottle of wine, than by making a pretty fabric gift bag?

Finished size
5½ x 13 x 2½ inches

Materials
• Cotton fat quarters:
  1 tan print
  2 purple batick
  2 green mottled
• Scraps burgundy batik
• 1 (¾–1⅛-inch) button
• Paper-backed fusible web
• 6-strand dark green embroidery floss
• Basic sewing supplies and equipment

Cutting
From tan print fat quarter:
• Cut one 17 x 15-inch rectangle for bag.

From purple batik fat quarters:
• Cut one 17 x 15-inch rectangle for lining.

• Trace template for grape (page 87) 16 times onto paper side of fusible web. Fuse onto wrong side of fabric. Cut out on traced lines for purple grape appliqués.

From green mottled fat quarters:
• Cut two 3 x 18-inch strips for ties.

• Trace template for leaf (page 87) twice, reversing one, onto paper side of fusible web. Cut out just outside traced lines. Fuse onto wrong side of fabric. Cut out on traced lines for grape leaf appliqués.

From scraps of burgundy batik:
• Trace template for grape (page 87) 10 times onto paper side of fusible web. Fuse onto wrong side of fabric. Cut out on traced lines for burgundy grape appliqués.

Assembly
Use ¼-inch seam allowance unless otherwise indicated. Press as you sew.

1. Position bag fabric right side up on flat surface with 15-inch edges as top and bottom of bag. With air-soluble marking pen, transfer grape cluster template to center front of bag with top of grape-cluster leaf 7 inches from top of bag.

2. Remove paper backing from appliqués and arrange within template lines, starting with leaves, then darker purple grapes and ending with lighter burgundy grapes. When satisfied with arrangement, fuse in place. Use 2 strands of dark green embroidery floss to embroider an outline or stem-stitch on tendrils.

3. Fold appliquéd bag in half (17-inch sides) with right sides together. Sew seam. Press seam open. Refold so seam runs down the center back of the bag (Figure 1). Press lightly at the bottom edge to make a crease at each side. Sew the bottom seam and use the tip of the iron to press the seam open.

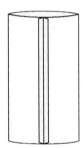

Figure 1

4. To box the bottom, fold bottom seam so seam line matches side creases on each side. Measure 1¼ inches from each tip and draw a line perpendicular to the seam (Figure 2). Sew on lines. Trim seams to ¼ inch. Turn bag right side out.

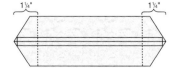

Figure 2

5. Press a ¼-inch hem at top edge of bag. Assemble lining in same manner as bag to this point, but do not turn right side out. Insert lining into bag with wrong sides of bag and lining together. Slipstitch top folded edges together to finish.

6. Sew strips for ties together at one short edge. Press seam open. Fold strip in half with right sides together and sew all around the raw edges, leaving a 2-inch opening. Trim corners and turn right side out. Press. Fold in seam allowance on opening and slipstitch opening closed.

7. Hold center of tie to center of back 3½ inches from top. Tack in place by sewing button through the tie and the bag. ⊗

Source: HeatnBond UltraHold iron-on adhesive from Therm O Web.

Sewing Tips

Batiks and hand-dyed fabric are often used for appliqué because there is such a variation of hues and shading in one piece of fabric, and because they resist fraying. The grapes look more realistic because each is slightly different.

When arranging pieces for fusible appliqué, a pin works well to pull appliqués into place.

Grape Cluster

Leaf

Grape

Appliquéd Wine Bag
Templates
Actual Size

Sewing Circle Etui

Design by Willow Ann Sirch

Sewing with special friends is always a treat. Be sure to let them know how special they are by gifting this small ornamental bag to each. You'll be thanked again and again.

Finished size
Approximately 8 inches in diameter x 3 inches tall, open

Materials
• Coordinating cotton fat quarters:
    1 outer fabric
    1 accent fabric 1
    1 accent fabric 2
• Scrap batting
• 4 yards coordinating cord

• Heavyweight art paper or card stock:
    1 sheet 16 x 16 inches for template A
    1 sheet 12 x 12 inches for template B
    2 sheets 8 x 10 inches for templates C and D
• Basic sewing supplies and equipment

Circle Templates
1. Enlarge templates (page 91) as indicated.

2. For full-size template A, fold 16 x 16-inch sheet of paper into quarters and crease. Unfold. Aligning tip of template at center of creases, trace arc, then flip template and trace again until a full circle has been traced.

3. For full-size template B, follow same procedure as in step 2, using 12 x 12-inch sheet of paper.

4. Trace templates C and D onto 8 x 10-inch sheets of paper. Transfer centerlines.

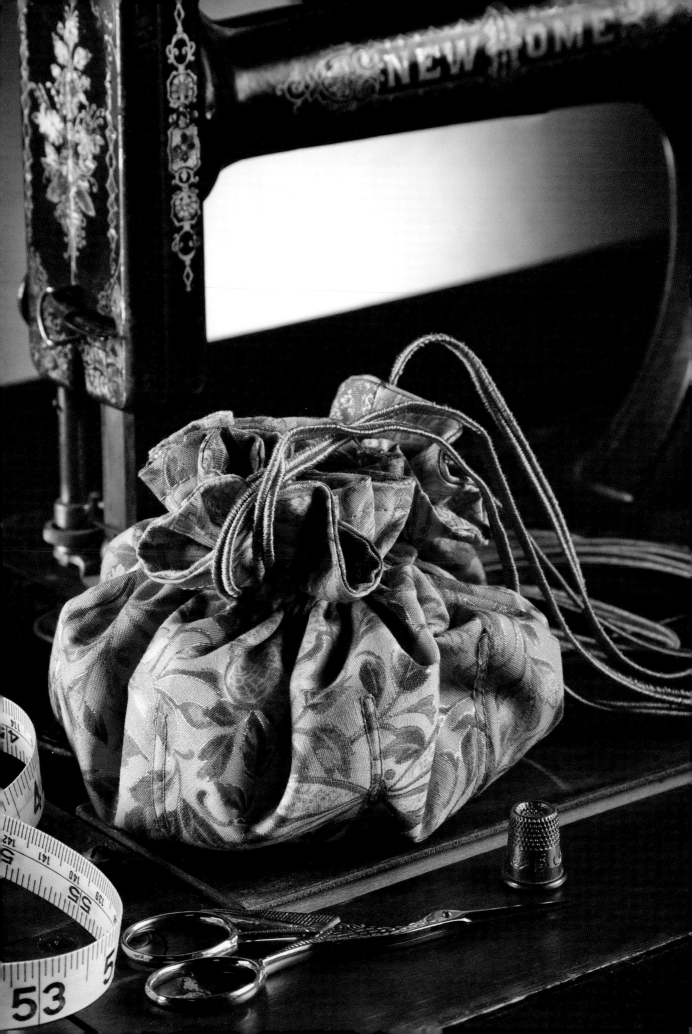

Cutting

From outer fabric fat quarter:

- Use template A to cut one circle.

- Use template B to cut one circle.

From accent fabric fat quarter:

- Cut accent fabric fat quarters in half making four 11 x 9-inch rectangles. With right sides together, sew an accent fabric 1 piece to an accent fabric 2 piece along one long edge; repeat to make two pieced rectangles. Press seams open.

- Use templates C and D to cut four larger and four smaller quarter-circles from pieced rectangles, aligning the centerline on template with seam line and cutting so fabrics will alternate when circle is sewn together. *Note: For the last one or two D quarter-circles, it will be necessary to use pieced scraps from fabric that is already cut away.*

From lightweight fusible interfacing:

- Use template A to cut one circle.

Assembly

Use ⅜-inch seam allowance unless otherwise stated. Press as you sew.

1. With right sides together, sew the four template C quarter-circles together. Repeat with template D quarter-circles. Press seams open.

2. With right sides together, pin the large outer-fabric circle to the large pieced circle. Sew outer edges together, leaving a 2-inch opening for turning. Turn right side out. Topstitch around outer edge.

3. Follow the same procedure as in step 2 to assemble the two smaller circles.

4. On large circle, stitch ¾ inch from topstitching. Sew again ¾ inch from that to form a casing for the drawstring cord.

5. Place large circle with pieced circle facing up. Place small circle on top of it with pieced circle facing up and arrange so accent fabrics alternate. Pin circles together in center. Double topstitch small circle to large circle using the seam on the small circle as a guide. Leave arc edges of circles open. *Note: By stitching up one side of a triangle and down the other side of the same triangle without lifting up the presser foot, this can be done in one long continuous line of sewing.*

6. Mark a 3-inch circle in the center of the small circle, beginning at the right edge of one triangle and ending at the left edge of the same triangle. Using the line as a guide, sew fabric layers together, leaving one triangle unsewn to create a small pointed pocket for sewing scissors.

7. Cut a 3-inch circle of outer fabric. Using a gathering stitch, baste the outer circle edge. Place scrap batting in circle center. Draw thread to gather fabric into a ball around batting, adding batting as needed. Hand-stitch to the inside center circle to form a pincushion.

8. Snip two small openings through outer fabric at opposite sides of casing. Apply seam sealant and let dry. Cut cord in half. Use small safety pin to insert one length through casing from each side and knot ends to form drawstrings. ⊗

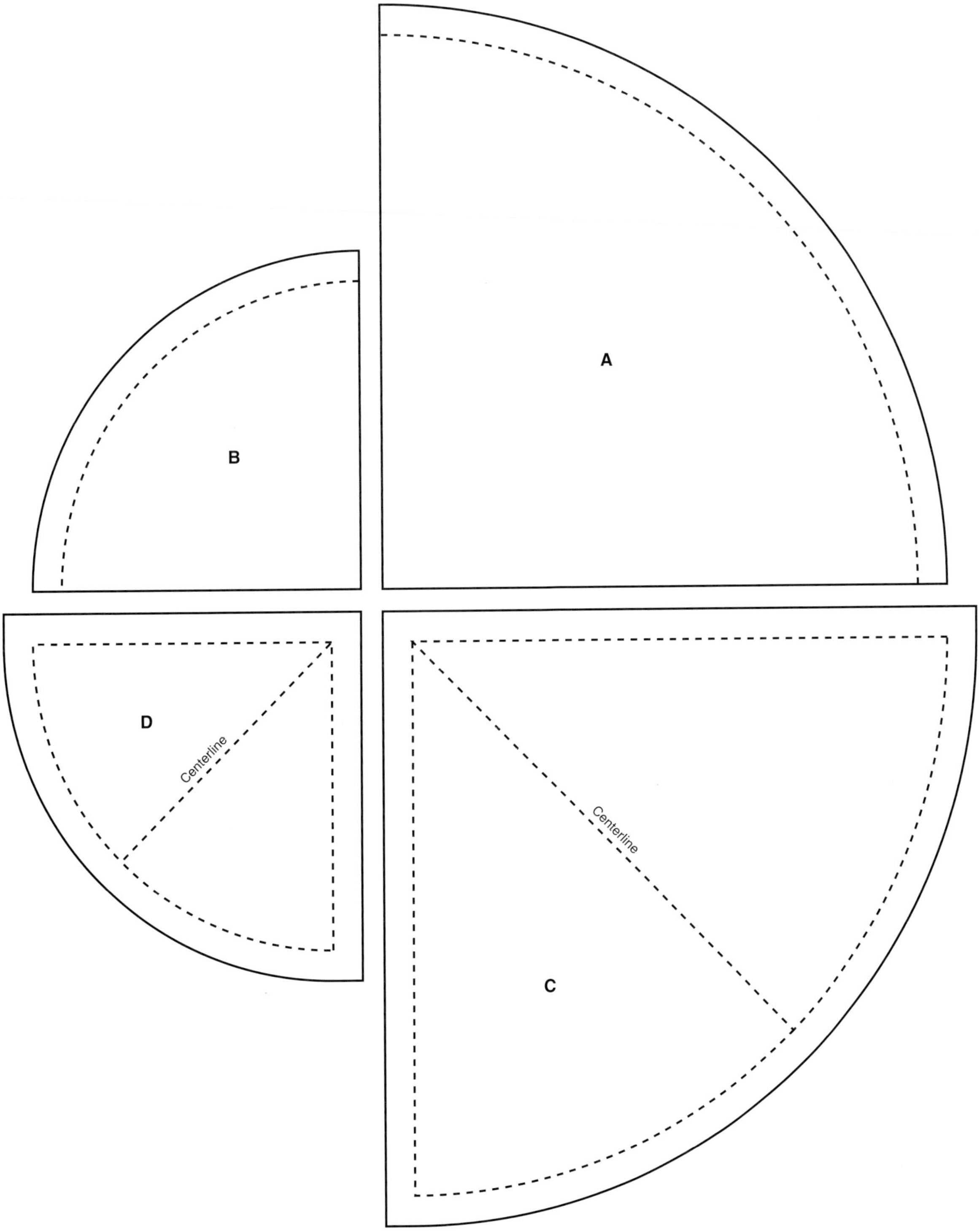

A

B

D

Centerline

Centerline

C

Sewing Circle Etui
Templates
Enlarge 200%

Patchwork Backpack

Design by Holly Daniels

Let your daughter, sister or best friend know how much you'll miss her while she is away by quilting this perfect travel size backpack. It's so easy to do, you'll want to make one for yourself too.

Finished size
Approximately 15 inches tall

Materials
- 8 fat quarters in light, medium and dark colors
- 16 x 44-inch piece backing fabric
- 16 x 44-inch piece lining fabric, or 2 fat quarters
- 16 x 40-inch piece thin quilt batting
- 6 sets ⁷⁄₁₆-inch silver eyelets
- Extra-large eyelet setter
- Large snap or magnetic snap closure
- Scraps fusible interfacing
- 4 x 4-inch square paper-backed fusible web
- 12 large-hole wooden beads
- Tube turner or knitting needle
- Basic sewing supplies and equipment

Cutting
From fat quarters:
- Cut one 6½ x 6½-inch square from one light fat quarter.

- Cut five 3½ x 3½-inch squares from each fat quarter (40 total).

- Cut one 3⅞ x 3⅞-inch square from each fat quarter, plus four additional 3⅞ x 3⅞-inch squares from two of the darker fat quarters (12 total). Cut eight of the squares in half diagonally to make 16 triangles.

- Cut one 4 x 4-inch square from a medium *or* dark fat quarter for heart appliqué.

- Cut two 2½ x 22-inch strips from one remaining fat quarter for straps.

- Using template (page 95), cut one bag bottom from a darker fat quarter.

- Cut and piece enough 2½-inch-wide strips from remaining fat quarters to equal 32 inches for binding.

- Cut and piece enough 1½-inch-wide strips from remaining fat quarters to equal 22 inches for ties. **Note:** *If desired, substitute purchased cord.*

From backing fabric:
- Cut a 15½ x 30½-inch rectangle.

- Using template (page 95), cut one bag bottom.

From lining fabric:
- Cut a 15½ x 30½-inch rectangle.

- Using template (page 95), cut one bag bottom.

From batting:
- Cut a 15½ x 30½-inch rectangle.

- Using template (page 95), cut one bag bottom.

Assembly

Use ¼-inch seam allowance unless otherwise stated. Sew with right sides together. Press as you sew.

1. Place one 3⅞-inch darker-color square into one corner of the 6½-inch square. Sew diagonally across smaller square. Trim away excess in seam allowance and press seam away from center (Figure 1). Sew remaining three 3⅞-inch dark-color squares to the remaining corners of 6½-inch square in same manner.

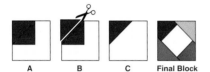

Figure 1

2. Trace heart appliqué (page 95) onto paper side of fusible web. Fuse to back of 4-inch square as directed by manufacturer. Let cool. Cut out heart on traced line. Remove paper backing and fuse to center of 6½-inch square. Machine-appliqué using blanket or satin stitch.

3. Sew triangles together in light/dark pairs (Figure 2). Press seams toward dark side. Sew two triangle units together with light fabrics toward center and press seam to right. Repeat with two more triangle units. Sew two double triangle units together to form a square. Make a second square with remaining triangle units.

Make 8   Make 2 blocks

Figure 2

4. Referring to Assembly Diagram, lay heart square and triangle squares on flat surface. Arrange 3½-inch squares as shown. ***Note:*** *Two squares will not be used.* Sew squares together in vertical rows. Press seams up in odd rows and down in even rows. Sew vertical strips together to form outer bag.

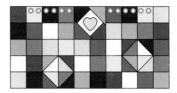

Patchwork Backpack
Assembly Diagram

5. Layer backing fabric, batting and outer fabric; pin or baste together. Using a variety of decorative machine stitches, stitch over seams to secure layers. Sew short sides of bag together to form a tube. Add decorative stitching over this seam as well.

6. Fold each strap in half lengthwise, right sides together, and sew to form long tubes. Turn right sides out. Press so seams are on center backs.

7. Layer backing, batting and fat-quarter bag bottom pieces with batting in middle and baste edges together. Mark front, back and ends of bag and of bottom with pins. With right sides together, pin bag bottom to bag, matching at pins and pleating bag at rounded corners to fit.

8. Insert raw edges of straps two patches apart in seam. Sew bottom to bag. Pin opposite ends of straps to top edge of bag next to each other with raw edges even. Sew through straps and outer bag to hold in place.

9. Sew lining fabric and attach bottom in same manner as for bag. Place lining in bag, wrong sides together.

10. Measure 2 inches from center top of bag and mark for placement of large snap or magnetic snap closure. Interface wrong side of lining at these points and attach snaps following manufacturer's instructions.

11. Sew binding strips together. Press seams. Fold strips in half lengthwise, wrong sides together, and press. Sew binding to right side of bag with raw edges even. Fold binding over raw edge and hand-stitch folded edge inside bag.

12. Follow manufacturer's instructions to attach six eyelets to each side of bag. Fold each strip for ties in half lengthwise, right sides together, and sew ½ inch from raw edge. Turn using a tube turner or knitting needle. Press. Thread ties through eyelets, draw up as desired and tie. Thread three wooden beads on each end of each tie; knot ends. Trim away excess fabric. ⊗

Source: Extra-large eyelets and eyelet setter by Prym Consumer USA Inc.

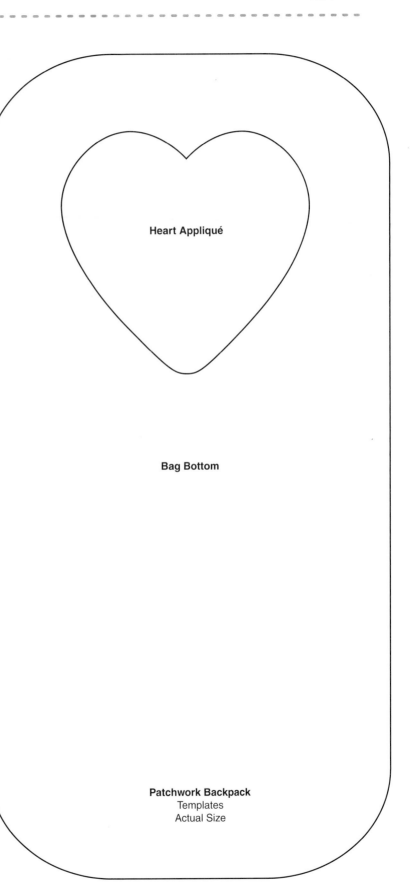

Heart Appliqué

Bag Bottom

Patchwork Backpack
Templates
Actual Size

On the Go Bag

Design by Missy Shepler

Making a padded pocket bag to protect a laptop computer is a great gift for a busy student or career person. Use pretty florals or conservative stripes to show the personality of the carrier. Our design uses covered seams to keep fabric lint away from sensitive electronics.

Finished size

17 x 14¼ x 2 inches

Materials

- Coordinating cotton fat quarters:
    2 for outer fabric
    2 for lining fabric
    1 for binding
- 1 yard 45-inch-wide cotton batting
- Optional: walking foot
- Basic sewing supplies and equipment

Project notes

Model project will fit a laptop that measures approximately 14 x 11 x 1½ inches. Measure your laptop before purchasing fabric. Adjust fabric quantities and measurements accordingly.

Machine-wash and dry fabrics. Press to remove wrinkles.

Quilting

1. Cut batting into four fat-quarter–size pieces. With wrong sides of fabrics toward batting, layer outer fabric, two layers of batting and lining fabric to create two quilt sandwiches for front and back of bag. Pin layers together.

2. On bag front sandwich, quilt entire sandwich. On bag back sandwich, mark quilting area as shown in Figure 1. Leave edge areas unquilted. Quilt as desired, leaving plenty of space between quilting lines so batting will remain puffy. *Note: A walking foot works well to tame the extra thickness and helps keep all layers aligned.*

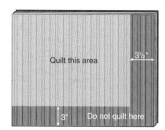

Quilt this area   3⅞"

3"   Do not quilt here

Figure 1

Cutting

Refer to Cutting Diagrams (page 98) to get the most out of fat-quarter yardage.

From quilted panels:

- Cut two 18 x 14½-inch rectangles for bag front and back.

- Cut two 1½ x 16-inch strips for handles.

- Cut one 2½ x 16-inch strip for power-cord flap.

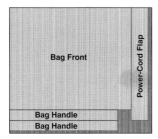
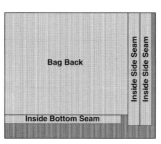
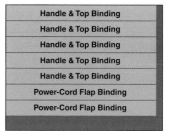

Padded Laptop Bag
Cutting Diagrams

From unquilted portion of lining fabric panel only:
- Cut one 1¼ x 17-inch strip for inside bottom seam.

- Cut two 1¾ x 16-inch strips for inside side seams.

From binding fabric:
- Cut seven 2¼ x 22-inch strips.

Assembly

Use ¼-inch seam allowance unless otherwise stated.

1. Join binding strips and apply to quilted power-cord flap along two short and one long side. *Note: Refer to Quick Quilt Binding on page 99.* Center long bound edge of power-cord flap along bottom inside edge of bag back. Stitch along unbound flap edge, close to unbound edge (Figure 2a). Flip bound edge of flap toward top of bag and stitch along unbound edge again ¼ inch from fold, encasing raw edge of flap in seam (Figure 2b).

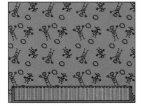

Figure 2a   Figure 2b

2. Apply binding to edges of quilted handle pieces. Center one handle on right side of bag front, placing handle ends 4¾ inches in from side edges and 3 inches from top edge. Stitch ends of handle securely to bag front, leaving handle unstitched ½ inch from bag top edge (Figure 3). Repeat with bag back and remaining handle.

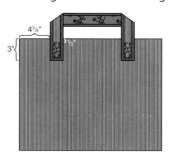

Figure 3

3. With bag front and back right sides together, stitch bottom seam. Press seam open. Press under ¼ inch along lengthwise edges of 1¼ x 17-inch unquilted lining strip for inside bottom seam. Place strip over bag bottom seam, encasing raw edges. Pin. Stitch through all layers along both sides of seam.

4. With bag front and back right sides together, stitch side seams. Press under ¼ inch along lengthwise edges of both 1¾ x 16-inch unquilted lining strips for inside side seams. Fold strips in half lengthwise, wrong sides together. Press again. Open folded strips. With right sides together,

align each strip raw edge with a stitched side seam. Stitch the strip to the side seam along the pressed ¼-inch fold of the strip, deepening the side seam to ½ inch (Figure 4). At bottom of bag, fold ¾-inch length of strip into seam, trimming strip, if necessary, before ending seam. Wrap strip around bag side seam and pin, folding under raw lengthwise edge along pressed line. Stitch through all layers.

5. Turn bag right side out and bind top bag edge with remaining binding. ⊗

Figure 4

Source: Warm & Natural quilt batting from The Warm Company.

Quick Quilt Binding

Binding a piece with corners

1. Join binding strips at short ends and press seams open to minimize bulk. Fold strip wrong sides together along the length and press.

2. Align the raw edges of the strip with the edge of the quilted piece. Pin if necessary. Machine-stitch ¼ inch along the edge of the piece. Stop and backstitch ¼ inch from the corner (Figure 1).

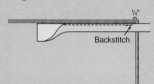

Figure 1

3. Remove the piece from the machine and snip threads. With the stitched strip at the top, fold the binding strip up so that folded binding edge is at a 45-degree angle with corner of quilted piece (Figure 2a). Fold binding strip back down, keeping the strip even with the edge of the quilt. Beginning stitching ¼ inch from the corner of the piece, stitch the binding with a ¼-inch seam allowance (Figure 2b). Stop stitching and backstitch ¼ inch from next corner.

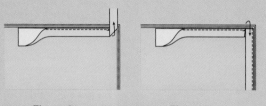

Figure 2a   **Figure 2b**

4. Repeat for all corners.

5. To finish, fold binding to the opposite side of the piece, covering the raw edges of the quilted panels. Blind-stitch along the binding fold.

Binding around a piece

1. If applying binding all around a piece, such as around bag top or around handle edges, join binding ends by layering one end of strip over the other. Using strip end as a guide, mark a line ½ inch from strip end. Trim strip on marked line and stitch strip ends right sides together with a ¼-inch seam allowance. Press seam open and press binding in half. Finish sewing binding to quilted pieces.

2. To finish, fold binding to the opposite side of the piece, covering the raw edges of the quilted panels. Blind-stitch along the binding fold.

Petite Purses

Design by Missy Shepler

These petite purses are perfect for presenting gift cards or other tiny treasures to someone special.

Finished size
5 x 4 x 1½ inches

Materials
• Cotton fat quarters*:
    1 for outer fabric
    1 for lining fabric
• 18 x 22 inches lightweight fusible interfacing
• Matching threads for twisted-cord handle
• 1 (½-inch) decorative button for purse flap
• Optional: snap or magnetic closure
• Basic sewing supplies and equipment

2 fat quarters will make 4 purses.

Cute Cords
If you have a top bobbin winder on your sewing machine, you can use it to quickly twist cords from thread and lightweight yarn. ***Note:*** *Designate a specific bobbin for this use, as this may distort bobbin edges and make them unsuitable for sewing purposes.*

1. Cut 12–15 (2-yard) lengths of thread. Holding the strands together, knot one end around the bobbin hole. Trim ends near knot to avoid tangles. Place bobbin on winder.

2. Hold threads taut but not tight, about 18 inches above the bobbin winder. Keep the remaining lengths of thread away from the section to be wound.

3. Turn bobbin winder on for 1–2 seconds, and then pause, working the twist up the thread. Allow threads to twist, but not kink together. Continue twisting thread in this way until the entire length of thread is twisted.

4. Holding the far end of twisted thread in one hand and using the other hand to keep thread taut, find the lengthwise center of the twisted strand. Bring the far end and the bobbin end of the strand together and remove the bobbin from the winder. Allow the folded strand to twist together, creating a thicker cord.

5. Treating the folded strand as one piece, continue twisting the strand. Find the lengthwise center and bring the strand ends together again, allowing the strand to twist on itself one more time. Knot the ends to secure.

Assembly

Use ¼-inch seam allowance unless otherwise stated. Sew right sides together.

1. Sew outer purse and purse sides together between points A and B (Figure 2). Finger-press purse bottom seam toward side pieces.

Figure 2

2. Sew sides to purse back from points C to A, taking care not to catch purse bottom in stitching. Sew sides to purse front from points B to D.

3. Clip corners and turn purse right side out. Finger-press seams away from purse sides.

4. Repeat steps 1 and 2 to construct the lining. *Note: If your machine has a needle-position option, move the needle one or two positions to the left while sewing the lining to make it slightly smaller for a better fit inside the purse.* Clip corners and trim seam allowances; press. Do not turn lining right side out.

5. Place flaps of outer purse and purse lining right sides together. Stitch flap curve from point C to point C. Clip curve and turn flap right side out, tucking lining inside purse. Press purse flap seam.

6. Turn under ¼ inch of outer purse and purse lining along top edges, creating a knife edge. Fold purse/lining sides and bottoms paper-bag style (Figure 3). Press to set folds. Hand-stitch top edge closed.

Cutting

From outer fabric fat quarter:

• Fuse interfacing to wrong side of fat quarter. Use template to cut one purse and two purse sides. Clip seam allowances on purse at points A, B and C, taking care not to clip into seam line (Figure 1). Transfer fold lines.

Figure 1

From lining fabric fat quarter:

• Use template to cut one purse and two purse sides.

Figure 3

7. Sew decorative button on purse flap. Attach desired closure to purse under flap, or secure flap with a length of twisted cord looped over the decorative button.

8. Stitch knotted ends of twisted cord to back of purse flap for handle, or loop a longer length of twisted cord under the purse flap and tack in place, making sure stitches don't show on the purse right side. ⊗

Sources: Fabric from Fig Tree Quilts by Moda; fusible interfacing from Pellon Consumer Products.

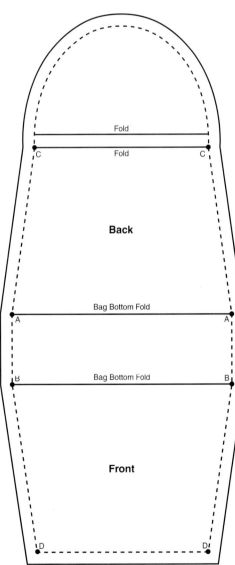

Petite Purses
Templates
Enlarge 200%

Compact Travel Bag

Design by Dorothy R. Martin

Surprise a friend with this pretty bag encased in a zippered wallet! The perfect item for unique purchases during a trip, this project is easy to make and sure to please.

Finished size
Closed wallet: 6 x 6¾ inches
Opened bag: Approximately 13 x 15 inches

Materials
• 5 cotton fat quarters:
    1 fabric (A) for wallet*
    2 fabric (B) for bag
    1 coordinating fabric (C) for contrast band
    1 coordinating fabric (D) for bag trim
      and straps
• ¼ yard heavyweight fusible interfacing
• 1 (20–22-inch) zipper

• Cotton or rayon machine-embroidery thread
• For optional machine-embroidered appliqué**:
    embroidery machine
    desired embroidery motifs
    tear-away stabilizer
• 1 hook-and-eye closure
• Open-toe appliqué or embroidery foot
    with tunnel bottom for zigzagged edges
• Optional embellishments:
    hot-fix crystals and applicator
    crystal buttons or charms for zipper tab
• Spray starch
• Basic sewing supplies and equipment

*If machine-embroidering appliqué, 2 fat quarters
   may be needed, depending on the size of the hoop.*
**Purchased appliqués may be substituted for
   machine embroidery.*

Cutting
From (A) fat quarter:
Trace wallet template (page 108) on fold to make full-size template. Transfer all markings.

• Use template to cut one wallet. ***Note:*** *If machine-embroidering the appliqués, refer to owner's manual to embroider motifs on lower portion of uncut fat quarter. Use template to cut out wallet, matching markings.*

• Cut one 16 x 7-inch rectangle for wallet lining.

From (B) fat quarters:
- Cut two 16 x 18-inch rectangles for bag front and back.

From (C) fat quarter:
- Cut two 16 x 4-inch strips for contrast bands.

From (D) fat quarter:
- Cut two 16 x 2-inch strips for trim.
- Cut two 16 x 1½-inch strips for handles.

From heavyweight interfacing:
- Cut one 16 x 7-inch piece for wallet.

Assembly

Use ½-inch seam allowance. Sew with right sides together, unless otherwise stated. Press seams as you sew.

1. Spray-baste 16 x 7-inch piece of interfacing to wrong side of wallet. If using purchased appliqués, sew appliqué to wallet at this time. Fuse the wrong side of the 16 x 7-inch lining fabric to the interfacing. Trim edges of all three layers even.

2. Using open-toe appliqué or embroidery foot with embroidery thread in needle and in bobbin, overcast edges with zigzag stitch set at 3.5W/.5L. Trim edge and re-stitch with settings of 4.0W/.5L for a smooth finish.

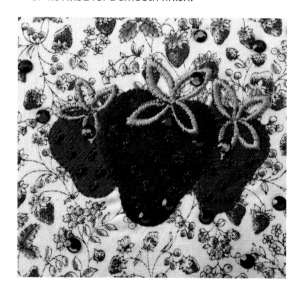

3. Fold wallet in half and measure length around the three sides (approximately 18 inches). Mark zipper with measured length. Zigzag-stitch over zipper teeth with a 5.0W/0L setting to create a new stop. Cut zipper ¼ inch below this point.

4. On the lining side of the wallet, beginning and ending at the center fold, pin the zipper in place so the teeth extend just beyond the zigzagged edges (Figure 1). Sew ¼ inch from zipper teeth, tucking under ends of zipper tape. Sew again ⅛ inch from teeth.

Figure 1

5. Sew bag front and back together along one 18-inch edge. Press seam open. Sew 16 x 2-inch trim strips (D) together along one short edge. Press seam open. Fold in half with wrong sides facing to make trim 1 inch wide. Press. Baste to right side of bag front/back, matching raw edges.

6. Press each long edge of each handle strip ½ inch to wrong side (Figure 2). Press strips in half lengthwise to form handles approximately ⅜ inch wide and topstitch edges. Referring to Figure 3 for placement, baste ends of handles to wrong sides of bag. With right sides together, sew remaining side of bag front and back together. Press seams open.

Figure 2

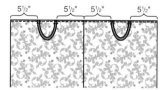

Figure 3

7. Sew bottom edge of bag. Press seam open. Fold bottom of bag, matching side and bottom seams to form a triangle. Measure along bottom seam line 3½ inches from point of triangle. Stitch at this point to box the bottom of bag (Figure 4). Trim seam allowance to 1 inch. Press.

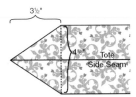

Figure 4

8. Sew short edges of contrast bands together. Press seams open. Sew band to top of bag, matching raw edges with right side of trim against wrong side of bag. Press seam up. Press under remaining raw edge of band ½ inch. With handles inside bag, pin folded edge of band to right side of bag and stitch, covering previous lines of stitching. Fold handles up and topstitch upper edge of band, including handles in stitching.

9. Press edges of bag from boxed bottom corner to top corner; topstitch close to pressed edge (Figure 5). **Note:** *Topstitched edges should measure approximately 2⅛ inches from side seams.* Press sides of bag together, grocery-bag style, to define the bottom. Press folds from corner to corner. Center and pin rectangle bottom of bag to inside of wallet. Stitch close to bottom folds. With wallet open flat, accordion-fold bag to fit inside wallet, pressing as you go. Add hook-and-eye closure between handles at bag top. Fold wallet and zip closed.

Figure 5

10. If desired, embellish with hot-fix crystals following manufacturer's instructions. Add crystal buttons or charms to zipper pull. ⊗

Sources: Fat quarters from G Street Fabrics; shirtmaker interfacing from Pellon Consumer Products; embroidery motifs from Martha Pullen; Ultra Solvy tear-away stabilizer and embroidery thread from Sulky of America; rhinestone hook-and-loop closure from Newark Dressmaker Supply; Lorna hot-fix embellishments and wand by Kandi Corp.

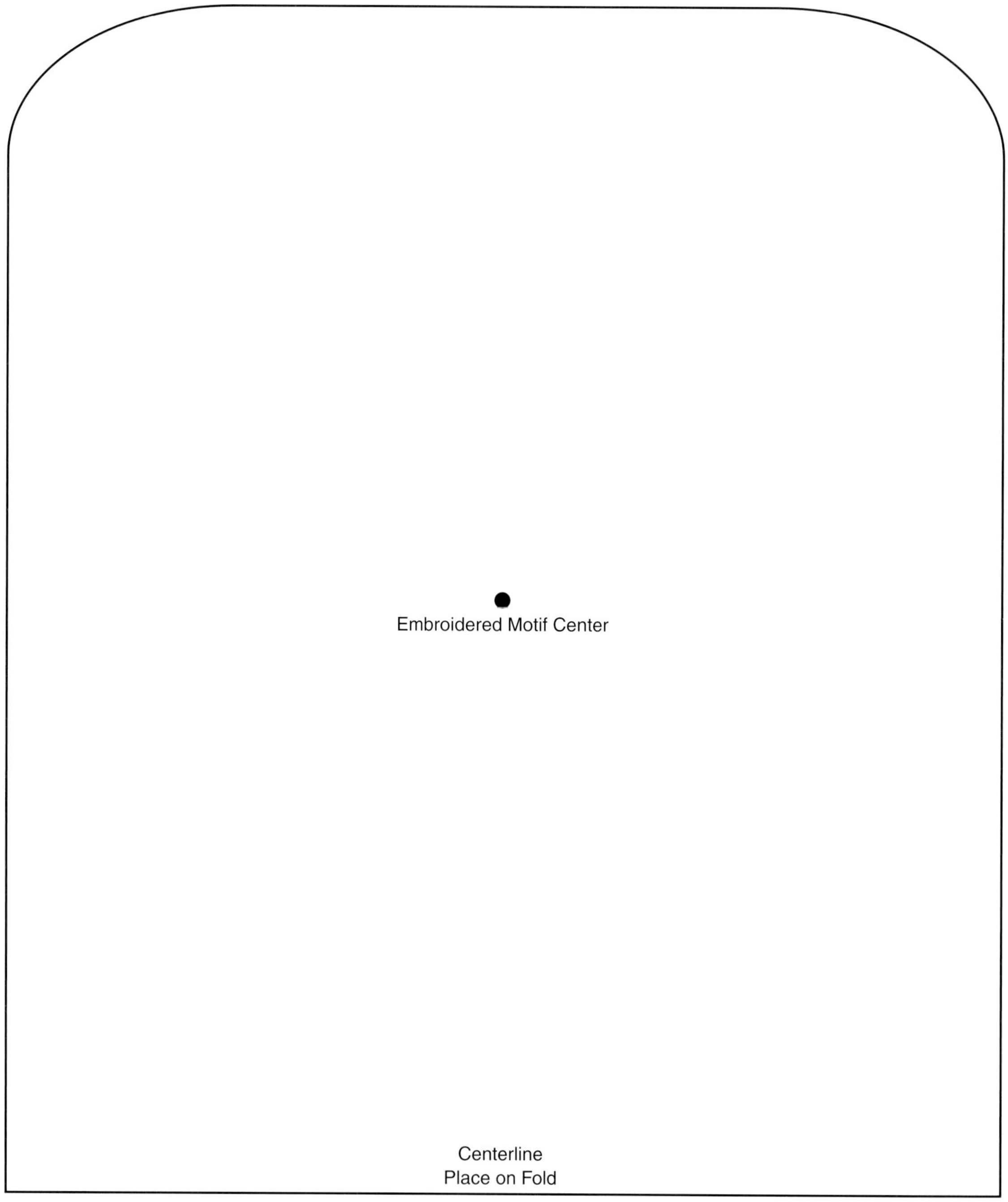

Embroidered Motif Center

Centerline
Place on Fold

Compact Travel Bag
Wallet Template
Actual Size

Sew Special Gift Bags

Design by Zoe Graul

One fat quarter will make two bags to be treasured or passed along. The more you make, the more variety you will have, and the faster they will go together.

Finished size
6½ x 7 x 4 inches, excluding handles

Materials
• 1 fat quarter Christmas print fabric
• Scrap coordinating fabric
• ⅓ yard 44/45-inch-wide unbleached muslin
• Needled cotton batting*
• 2 yards ⅜-inch-wide grosgrain ribbon
• 16 inches ⅜-inch-wide decorative flat trim
• 10 (¾-inch) assorted buttons
• 4 x 6-inch piece cardboard or plastic canvas
• Rubber stamp, fabric paint, small paintbrush
• Fabric marker
• Basic sewing supplies and equipment
* *Batting requirement is the same as for the muslin. A craft bag of Warm & Natural batting (34 x 45 inches) will make 6 bags.*

Project notes
Cut fabrics using rotary cutter and mat. If using more than one fat quarter to make multiple bags, layer fabrics and batting to cut. Do not cut through more than two layers of batting at one time.

Cutting for two bags
From fat quarter:
Note: Refer to cutting diagram for fat quarter.

- Cut two 6½ x 4-inch bottoms.

- Cut four 4 x 7-inch sides.

- Cut two 6½ x 7-inch backs.

- Cut two 6½ x 2½-inch lower fronts.

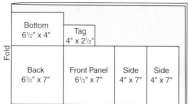

Fat Quarter

Muslin & Batting (Double Layer)
Repeat for second bag

Sew Special Gift Bags
Cutting Diagrams

From scraps of coordinating fabric:
- Cut two 3 x 3-inch upper left side squares.

- Cut two 3 x 3-inch lower left side squares.

- Cut two 4 x 2½-inch tags. Cut one end of each tag on a 1-inch diagonal across two corners (Figure 1).

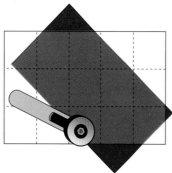

Figure 1

From muslin and batting:
Note: Refer to cutting diagram for muslin and batting.

- Cut two 6½ x 4-inch bottoms.

- Cut four 4 x 7-inch sides.

- Cut two 6½ x 7-inch backs.

- Cut two 6½ x 7-inch front panels.

- Cut two 4 x 2½-inch tags. Cut one end of each tag on a 1-inch diagonal (see Figure 1 for coordinating scrap tag).

From ribbon:
- Cut six 12-inch lengths.

Stamping
1. Apply fabric paint to rubber stamp using paintbrush; immediately press stamp onto muslin front panel, applying even pressure. Carefully remove stamp.

2. Follow paint manufacturer's instructions for drying, setting and cleanup.

Assembly for each bag
Use ¼-inch seam allowance unless otherwise stated. Press as you sew.

1. With right sides together, sew an upper left side square to a lower left side square using ½-inch seam allowance; press. Sew pieced left side to left edge of stamped front panel, right sides together. Press. Sew this assembly to lower front to complete pieced front.

2. Layer each front, back, side fabric piece with corresponding muslin piece, sandwiching batting piece between; pin-baste layers together. Layer bottom fabric piece with corresponding batting piece and pin-baste.

3. On back and both side pieces, using a regular-length stitch, sew across each top through all layers ¼ inch from edges; then sew vertically down the center of each piece to quilt. On bottom, sew lengthwise through center of piece only to quilt.

4. On front, sew across top as for back and sides. Stitch-in-the-ditch between front panel and pieced left side, and between upper and lower left side squares. Pin flat trim over seam joining lower front and upper front assembly, and stitch in place.

5. Square up pieces as needed, trimming ends of flat trim; baste layers of each piece together. Apply seam sealant to ends of trim; let dry.

6. With wrong sides together, sew sides to front and back, ending stitching ¼ inch above bottom edge; sew bottom to front, back and sides, matching raw edges. Remove basting threads.

7. Trim cardboard to fit inside bottom of bag, if needed, and cover with muslin bottom piece, turning ends under and securing on bottom of cardboard. Slide cardboard into bag.

8. Sew a button on front at intersection of left side pieces and front panel. Fold under ends of two 12-inch lengths of ribbon and tack inside bag 1–1½ inches from sides of bag for handles. Sew buttons on outside of bag to secure ends of ribbons.

9. Write desired message on muslin tag using fabric marker. Layer tag pieces with fat quarter fabric on bottom, batting in middle and muslin on top, message side up. Pin to secure.

10. Fold a 12-inch length of ribbon in half. Tuck fold between layers at end of tag. Stitch around tag, catching ribbon fold in stitching. Apply seam sealant to ends of ribbon; let dry. Tie tag to bag. ⊗

Heart of the Home

Family, friends and food—these are intertwined to create festive, fun occasions. Whether your gift-giving needs involve fine seasonal or holiday cuisine, simple Italian pasta spreads with bread and wine, an effortless tea and toast, or a pick-me-up coffee break, you'll want to try your hand at whipping up these fun, food-inspired creations from fat quarters.

Coffee, Tea or Me?

Designs by Carolyn Vagts

Make an adorable apron gift set to give to a special someone who can answer that celebrated question: coffee, tea or me?

Finished sizes

Apron: Fits average adult
Pot Holder: 9 x 9 inches, excluding hanging loop
Chef Hat: 21½ inches in circumference
Oven Mitten: Fits average adult
Coaster: 5 x 5 inches

Materials

• Cotton fat quarters:
  4 coffee-bean print
  2 coffee-cup print
  1 cream (to match tea towel)
  2 black solid
• 27½ x 20-inch cream-color tea towel for apron
• Scraps batiks for appliqué:
  black for coffee cup
  batik tan for coffee
  batik gray for steam
• Scraps batting
• 22 x 36 inches needlepunched
  insulated batting
• Paper-backed fusible web
• Basic sewing supplies and equipment

Apron & Pot Holders

Cutting

From tea towel:
• Referring to Apron Cutting Diagram on page 116, cut corners from one end of tea towel.

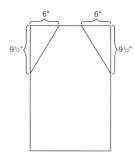

Coffee, Tea or Me?
Apron Cutting Diagram

From coffee-bean print fat quarters:
• Cut five 2½ x 22-inch strips for ties.

• Cut two 9 x 22-inch rectangles. Layer needlepunched insulated batting between rectangles; quilt as desired. Cut two 9 x 9-inch squares for pot holders from quilted rectangles.

From coffee-cup print fat quarters:
• Cut two 9 x 14-inch rectangles for apron pockets.

• Cut two 9 x 14-inch rectangles for pot holder pockets.

From black solid fat quarter:
• Cut five 2½ x 22-inch strips for binding.

From scraps batiks for appliqué:
• Using appliqué templates on page 118, individually trace steam, coffee cup and coffee onto paper side of fusible web, leaving space between. Cut out just outside traced lines. Fuse onto appropriate fabric scraps. Cut out on traced lines.

From scrap batting:
• Cut two 9 x 7-inch rectangles for pot holders.

Assembly
Use ¼-inch seam allowance. Sew with right sides together, unless otherwise stated. Press as you sew.

1. Fold each apron pocket in half with right sides together. Sew around three sides, leaving an opening for turning (Figure 1). Turn right side out; press.

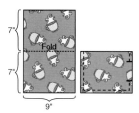

Figure 1

2. Position pockets on apron front approximately 6 inches from bottom of apron and 1½ inches apart. Topstitch side and bottom edges.

3. Remove paper backing from appliqué pieces and fuse in place on apron front, using photo as a guide for placement.

4. Sew 2½-inch-wide coffee-bean print strips together on the bias to make one long strip for ties. Press in half lengthwise, wrong sides together. Open and press raw edges to center crease; refold to make ties. Referring to Figure 2, pin ties to apron. Beginning at one end of tie, topstitch folded edge closed, continuing to opposite end and catching apron in stitching. Knot tie ends to finish.

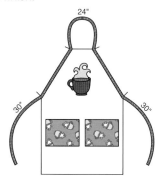

Figure 2

5. For each pot holder, fold pocket in half over scrap batting with wrong sides together. Free-motion sew to secure layers. Sew pocket to pot holder using a scant ¼-inch seam allowance (Figure 3).

Figure 3

6. Sew black binding strips together on the bias to make one long strip. Press in half with wrong sides together. Cut strip in half. With raw edges even and right sides together, sew each strip around edges of one pot holder, leaving a 4-inch tail for loop (Figure 4).

Figure 4

7. Fold binding strips over raw edges of pot holders and hand-stitch or topstitch into place. Topstitch extended strips for loops, then fold ends back onto pot holders and sew in place with zigzag stitch.

Chef Hat

Cutting
From cream fat quarter:
• Enlarge chef hat template (page 119) as indicated. Cut one on double fold.

From coffee-bean print fat quarters:
• Cut one 22 x 9½-inch rectangle for band.

From scrap batting:
• Cut one 22 x 4½-inch rectangle for band.

Assembly
Use ¼-inch seam allowance (included in templates). Sew with right sides together; press seams as you sew.

1. Make a gathering stitch around chef hat ¼ inch from edge. Pull threads to gather to approximately 12 inches in diameter.

2. Layer batting rectangle on wrong side of coffee-bean print rectangle with top and side edges even. Fold unit into a tube, right sides together, and sew 9½-inch edges together (Figure 5). Press bottom edge of tube under ¼ inch.

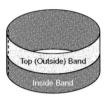

Figure 5

3. Tuck hat inside top edge of band, matching raw edges. Adjust gathers to fit band. Pin and stitch in place. Press seam toward band.

4. Turn hat right side out. Fold extended band to inside over batting and hand-stitch in place over seam line.

Oven Mitten & Coasters

Cutting
Layer needlepunched insulated batting between two coffee-bean print fat quarters. Quilt as desired.

From quilted coffee-bean print:
• Enlarge oven mitten template (page 119) as indicated. Cut two mittens.

• Cut four 5 x 5-inch squares for coasters.

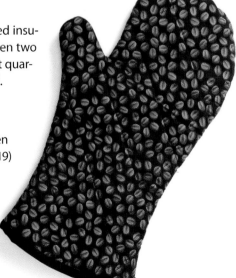

From black fat quarter:
• Cut five 2½ x 22-inch strips for binding.

Assembly

Use ¼-inch seam allowance (included in templates). Sew with right sides together; press seams as you sew.

1. Sew mitten pieces together, leaving top edge open. Clip curves. Turn right side out.

2. Press one 2½ x 22-inch black binding strip in half lengthwise with wrong sides together. With raw edges even and right sides together, sew strip around open edge of mitten, turning ends under.

Coffee, Tea or Me?
Appliqué Templates
Actual Size

3. Fold binding to inside of mitten and hand-stitch in place.

4. Using one black binding strip for each square, follow same procedure to bind edges of 5 x 5-inch squares for coasters. ⊗

Sources: Fabric from Hoffman California Fabrics; Insul-Bright needlepunched insulated batting from The Warm Company.

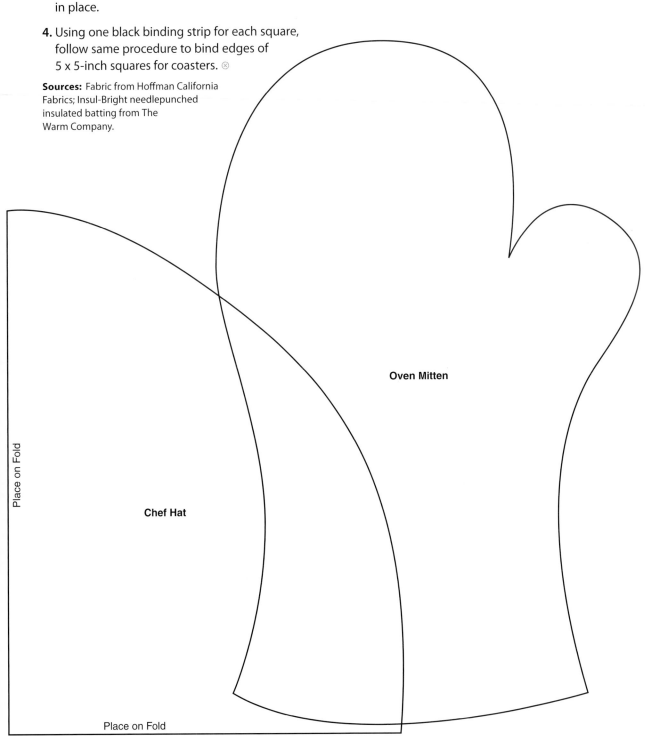

Place on Fold

Chef Hat

Oven Mitten

Place on Fold

Coffee, Tea or Me?
Templates
Enlarge 200%

Posy Cozy & Coasters

Designs by Chris Malone

Try planning an afternoon tea party for your next sewing guild meeting. They'll love to sew this appliquéd floral tea cozy and matching coasters.

Finished sizes
Cozy: 14½ x 11½ inches
Coaster: 4½ x 4½ inches

Materials
• Cotton fat quarters:
   4 coordinating light tan prints
   1 dark tan print for basket appliqué
    and coaster backings and borders
   1 green print
   1 red print
• Batting:
   2 (11½ x 14½-inch) rectangles
   4 (5 x 5-inch) squares
• 1 yard ⅛-inch piping cord
• 1 yard light tan single-fold bias tape
• Tan buttons:
   4 (¾-inch)
   4 (½-inch)
• Paper-backed fusible web
• Basic sewing supplies and equipment

Cutting
From four coordinating light tan print fat quarters:
• Cut two 6 x 7½-inch rectangles from each for tea cozy front and back.

• Cut two 11½ x 14½-inch rectangles from *one of the four* for tea cozy lining.

• Cut one 4 x 4-inch square from each for coaster fronts.

From dark tan print fat quarter:
• Cut four 5 x 5-inch squares for coaster backing.

• Cut eight 1 x 4-inch strips and eight 1 x 5-inch strips for coaster borders.

• Trace basket template (page 123) onto paper side of fusible web. Cut out just outside traced lines. Fuse onto wrong side of fabric. Cut out on traced lines.

From green print fat quarter:
• Cut two 1⅛ x 20-inch bias strips for piping.

• Trace template for tea cozy leaf (page 123) four times onto paper side of fusible web. Fuse onto wrong side of fabric. Cut out on traced lines.

• Trace template for coaster leaf (page 123) eight times, reversing four, onto paper side of fusible web. Fuse onto wrong side of fabric. Cut out on traced lines.

From red print fat quarter:
• Trace template for tea cozy flower (page 123) three times onto paper side of fusible web. Cut out just outside traced lines. Fuse onto wrong side of fabric. Cut out on traced lines.

• Trace template for coaster flower (page 123) four times onto paper side of fusible web. Cut out just outside traced lines. Fuse onto wrong side of fabric. Cut out on traced lines.

Assembly

Use ¼-inch seam allowance and sew right sides together unless otherwise indicated. Press as you sew.

1. Sew tea cozy front/back rectangles together in pairs along short edges. Press seams. Sew two pairs together to make a tea cozy front and a back, matching seams. Press.

2. Remove paper backing from tea cozy appliqué pieces and fuse in place on tea cozy front, using photo as a guide for placement. Blanket-stitch edges of all appliqués by hand or machine.

3. Fold tea cozy back in half. Using a dinner plate or similar object as a template, round the top corners (Figure 1).

Figure 1

4. Using tea cozy back as a pattern, cut tea cozy front, both tea cozy lining pieces and both 11½ x 14½-inch batting rectangles to match.

5. Place one cozy lining wrong side up with one batting piece on top. Smooth the cozy front in place with right side up; pin. Machine-baste all around just inside seam allowance. Repeat with cozy back.

6. On cozy front, sew a ¾-inch button to center of each flower, sewing through all layers. On cozy back, sew a ¾-inch button to center of patchwork back through all layers.

7. Join bias strips with a diagonal seam (Figure 2). Trim seam to ¼ inch and press open.

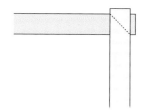

Figure 2

8. Wrap piping cord with bias strips and sew close to cord using a zipper foot. With raw edges even, pin piping to curved edge of cozy front. Machine-baste close to cord.

9. Pin cozy front and back together with right sides facing and raw edges even. Stitching from the wrong side of the cozy front so you can see the basting, stitch the layers together just inside the previous stitching line. Serge or zigzag seam edges to finish. Turn right side out.

10. Unfold bias tape and turn under short end ¼ inch. Beginning at back raw edge of cozy, sew tape to lower edge, stitching in the fold line with the raw edges even (Figure 3). Overlap end and trim excess. Wrap bias tape over raw edge to inside of cozy and slipstitch in place.

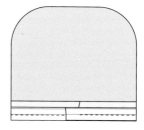

Figure 3

11. Referring to photo for placement, fuse one coaster flower and two coaster leaves to each coaster front, taking care to keep each motif ⅝ inch from the outside edge. Blanket-stitch around appliqué pieces by hand or machine.

12. Sew a 4-inch border strip to each side of an appliquéd front; press seams outward. Sew a

5-inch border strip to the top and bottom; press seams outward.

13. Pin coaster front and back, right sides together, to a 5-inch batting square. Sew around edges, leaving a 2½-inch opening on one side. Trim corners. Trim batting close to seam to reduce bulk. Turn right side out.

14. Fold in seam allowance on opening and slipstitch closed. Stitch in the ditch on front of coaster to quilt. Sew a ½-inch button to center of each flower through all layers. ⊗

Sources: Soft & Bright needled polyester batting from The Warm Company; HeatnBond Lite iron-on adhesive from Therm O Web.

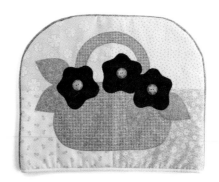

Sewing Tip

The blanket-stitch finish for appliqués can be applied by hand or machine. Use matching thread or floss for a subtle effect, or all black for a folk-art look.

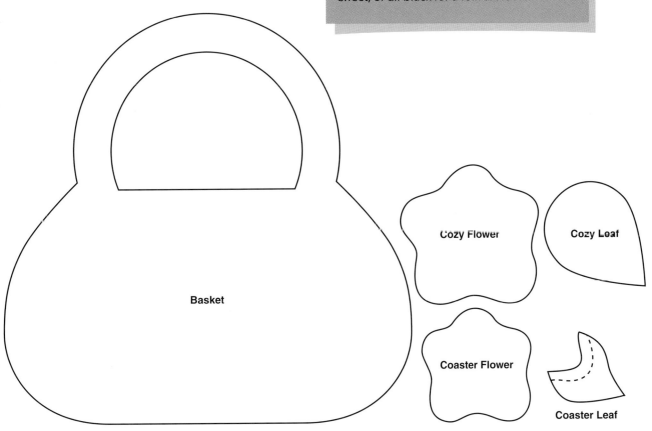

Basket

Cozy Flower

Cozy Leaf

Coaster Flower

Coaster Leaf

Posy Cozy & Coasters
Templates
Enlarge 200%

Cookie Tray Set

Designs by Lynn Weglarz

Here's the perfect last-minute hostess gift. It is so quick and easy to make, you even have time to fill the cookie tray with homemade cookies!

Finished sizes

Cookie Tray: 8 x 8 x 3 inches
Bottle Bag: 16¾ x 7¾ inches
Bread Bag: 20¾ x 7½ inches
Trivet: 10¾-inch octagon

Materials

- 4 coordinating fat quarters:
   1 dark solid
   1 light small print
   1 stripe
   4 figured print
- 1 yard cotton batting
- 4⅓ yards ⅛–¼-inch-wide ribbon
- ¼ yard stiff nonwoven double-sided fusible interfacing
- 1 package double-fold bias tape
- Lightweight fusible tape
- Teflon press cloth
- Basic sewing supplies and equipment

Cutting

From dark solid fat quarter:
- Cut one 14 x 14-inch square for cookie tray bottom.
- Cut four 3¼ x 3¼-inch squares for trivet patchwork.

From light small print fat quarter:
- Cut four 3¼ x 3¼-inch squares for trivet patchwork.
- Cut four 2¾ x 2¾-inch squares for corners of trivet patchwork.

From stripe fat quarter:
- Cut one 16 x 6-inch rectangle for bottle bag cuff.
- Cut three 1½ x 22-inch strips for trivet border.

From figured print fat quarters:
- Cut one 14 x 14-inch square for cookie tray top.
- Cut one 16 x 17¾-inch rectangle for bottle bag.
- Cut two 8 x 22-inch rectangles for bread bag.
- Cut one 5 x 5-inch square for trivet center front.
- Cut one 12 x 12-inch rectangle for trivet backing.

From cotton batting:
- Cut one 14 x 14-inch square for cookie tray.
- Cut two 12 x 12-inch squares for trivet.

From stiff nonwoven double-sided fusible interfacing:
- Cut one 8 x 8-inch square for cookie tray.

Assembly

Use ¼-inch seam allowance unless otherwise stated. Press as you sew.

1. Fold, quarter and gently press cookie tray bottom and 8 x 8-inch square of interfacing. Use Teflon press cloth to fuse interfacing to wrong side of bottom, matching fold lines. Center 14 x 14-inch square of batting over interfaced square. With wrong sides together, center cookie tray top over batting and fused square. Pin together through all layers.

2. On bottom, chalk a line around stiff interfacing. Sew through all layers (Figure 1).

Figure 1

3. Use a ruler to chalk corner lines (Figure 2). Stitch corners and cut out, leaving ⅛-inch seam allowance (Figure 3). Using a small zigzag stitch, sew all raw edges together.

Figure 2   **Figure 3**

4. Cut eight 9-inch lengths of ribbon. Baste one ribbon end at each corner of cookie tray (Figure 4). Bind edges of tray with bias tape, catching ends of ribbons in stitching. Tie ribbons in bows to form sides of tray.

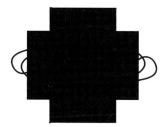

Figure 4

5. For bottle bag, sew cuff to bag with right sides together along one 16-inch side. Press seam toward bag. This will be the top of the bag. Baste two 12-inch lengths of ribbon 5 inches from the cuff seam. Fold bag in half with right sides together and fabric cuff extended. Stitch side and bottom seams, catching ends of ribbons in stitching.

6. Match bottom seam with side seams and make a line at right angles to the seam and 1½ inches from each point. Stitch on these lines to square the bottom of the bag (Figure 5).

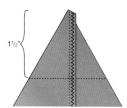

Figure 5

7. Press under a ¼-inch hem on raw edge of cuff. Fold cuff to inside of bag. Press. Topstitch hemmed edge of cuff in place, taking care not to catch ribbon ties in stitching. Turn right side out. Insert bottle and tie ribbons around neck of bottle to present as a gift.

8. With right sides together, sew bread bag pieces as shown in Figure 6 leaving 1½-inch open at top of bag. Trim corners. Press seams open. Press top edge under ¼ inch; fold ¾ inch to inside of bag and press. Stitch to form casing. Turn right side out. Thread a 30-inch length of ribbon through casings from one direction

and knot ends together. Repeat with a second 30-inch length of ribbon, threading through casing from opposite direction to make drawstrings.

Figure 6

9. For trivet, place one 3¼ x 3¼-inch dark solid and one light small print square with right sides together. Draw a line from one corner to the other. Mark a diagonal line ¼ inch on each side of the first line. Stitch on these lines, and then cut on the first corner-to-corner line to make two pieced squares. Press seams toward one side. Repeat with remaining 3¼-inch squares. Trim each pieced square to measure 2¾ x 2¾ inches.

10. Sew pieced squares together in pairs with light triangles in centers. Sew a joined pair on each side of the 5 x 5-inch trivet center-front square (Figure 7). On each end of the remaining joined pairs, sew a 2¾-inch light-print square. Sew this strip across the top and bottom of the trivet front unit.

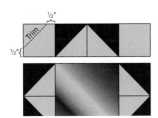

Figure 7

11. Again referring to Figure 7, trim corners of trivet front unit. With right sides together, sew a 1½-inch trivet border strip across top of the front unit and trim, allowing ends of strip to extend ½ inch beyond edges of trivet front (Figure 8). Repeat across bottom edge and both sides of front. Press seams to one side. Finish adding strips to the corners (Figure 9). Trim away excess fabric from strips.

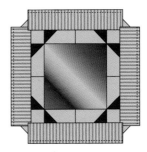

Figure 8

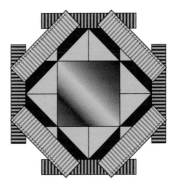

Figure 9

12. Layer trivet front on top of the two 12 x 12-inch batting squares and trim batting to fit. Place trivet backing square and trivet front right sides together; trim backing to fit front. Sew all layers together, leaving a 4-inch opening on one straight edge. Turn and slipstitch opening closed. Stitch on front close to border and just inside center front square to quilt. ⊗

Source: Warm and Natural cotton batting and Steam-A-Seam2 fusible tape from The Warm Company.

Poinsettia Table Runner

Design by Phyllis Dobbs

Bring the outside inside with this sure-to-please table runner made in holiday brights.

Finished size

42 x 11 inches, excluding trim

Materials

- Fat quarters:
  - 3 light green tonal print
  - 1 dark green tonal print
  - 1 red tonal print
- ⅓ yard 60-inch-wide cotton batting
- ¼ yard paper-backed fusible web
- 16 green E beads
- 24 inches red-and-green beaded trim
- Basic sewing supplies and equipment

Cutting

From light green tonal print fat quarters:

- Cut three 12½ x 6-inch rectangles.

- Cut two 21½ x 11½-inch rectangles for backing.

From dark green tonal print fat quarter:

- Cut three 12½ x 6-inch rectangles.

From red tonal print fat quarter:

- Cut two 3¾ x 11½-inch rectangles.

- Apply fusible web to wrong side of fabric following manufacturer's instructions. Trace and cut out four poinsettia appliqués using template on page 130.

Assembly

Use ¼-inch seam allowance. Sew with right sides together, unless otherwise stated. Press seams to darker fabrics as you sew.

1. Sew each light green 12½ x 6-inch rectangle to a dark green 12½ x 6-inch rectangle along one long edge. Sew light/dark green units together on short edges, alternating light/dark color placement. Sew red 3½ x 11½-inch rectangles to ends of light/dark green unit (Figure 1).

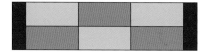

Figure 1

2. Referring to photo for placement, arrange poinsettia appliqués on runner. Trim the two outer poinsettias even with edges of runner. Stitch around remaining edges of appliqués using satin stitch. Sew four green E beads in center of each appliqué.

3. Sew short edges of the two backing rectangles together to make a 42½ x 11½-inch rectangle. Layer the runner top and backing with right sides together on top of batting. Trim batting the same size. Pin the three layers together.

4. Cut bead trim to fit across each end of runner between seam allowances and insert header between runner top and backing. ***Note:** Take*

Don't limit this festive table runner to the kitchen or dining room. Add or remove the light/dark green units to adjust the length by 12-inch increments to customize this runner for any room of the house.

care that beads are free from stitching line. Sew runner together around edges, leaving a 6-inch opening along one long edge (without an appliqué) for turning. Turn right side out and press. Hand-stitch opening closed.

5. Baste table runner layers together. Quilt around poinsettias and along seam lines on green fabrics, quilting two rows ⅛ inch apart on inside seams and around outer edges. ⊗

Sources: Cotton batting and Steam-A-Seam2 fusible web from The Warm Company; red and green bead trim #IR1781 from Expo International Inc.

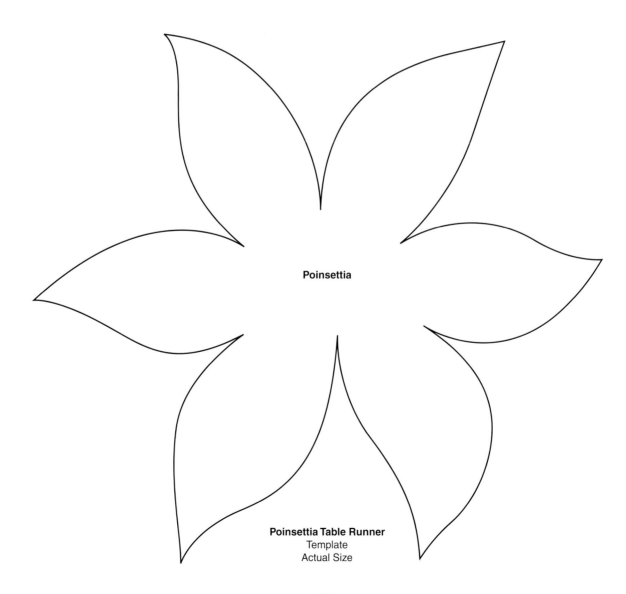

Poinsettia

Poinsettia Table Runner
Template
Actual Size

Summer Delight Runner

Design by Patsy Moreland

A simple-to-sew quilted table runner accented with yo-yos is a great gift to show your appreciation for a special holiday dinner.

Finished size
12 x 32 inches

Materials
• Coordinating cotton fat quarters:
    1 floral or fruit print
    1 blue print
    1 brown print
    1 light green print
    1 green print
    2 mottled prints for borders and strips
• 1 yard multicolored fusible bias tape to coordinate with fabric
• 12 x 32-inch piece craft batting
• Small yo-yo maker (1¼-inch finished size)
• Basic sewing supplies and equipment

Cutting
From floral print fat quarter:
• Cut two 4½ x 4½-inch squares on wrong side of fabric.

• Cut two 8½ x 4½-inch rectangles on right side of fabric.

• Following yo-yo manufacturer's instructions, cut squares to make six small yo-yos.

• Cut two 2½ x 22-inch strips for backing.

From blue print fat quarter:
• Cut three 4½ x 4½-inch squares.

• Cut two 2½ x 22-inch strips for backing.

From brown print fat quarter:
• Cut two 4½ x 4½-inch squares.

• Cut two 2½ x 22-inch strips for backing.

From light green print fat quarter:
• Cut one 4½ x 4½-inch square.

• Cut two 2½ x 22-inch strips for backing.

From green print fat quarter:
• Cut two 6½ x 4½-inch squares.

• Cut two 2½ x 22-inch strips for backing.

From mottled print fat quarters for borders and strips:
• Cut two 2½ x 10½-inch (F) strips.

• Cut one 2½ x 30½-inch (G) strip, piecing as needed.

• Cut two 2½ x 34½-inch (H) strips, piecing as needed.

Assembly

Use ¼-inch seam allowance. Sew with right sides together, unless otherwise stated. Press seams as you sew.

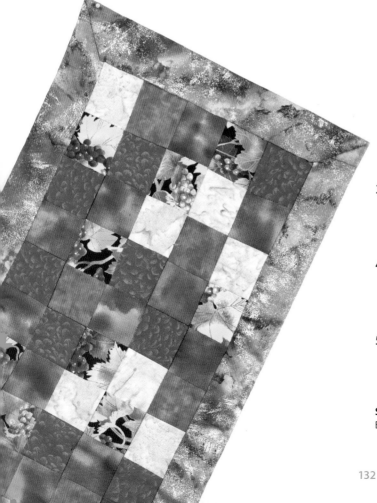

1. Referring to Assembly Diagrams, piece together strips 1 and 2. Sew strips 1 and 2 to edges of G strip. Sew F strips to ends of pieced unit. Sew H strips across top and bottom edges.

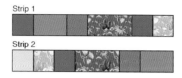

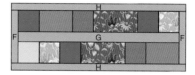

Summer Delight Runner
Assembly Diagrams

2. For backing, sew 2½-inch-wide strips together in random patterns. Cut across seams at 2½-inch intervals (Figure 1). Sew strips back together to form pieced backing of 15 rows of five blocks each.

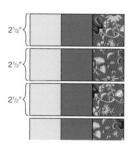

Figure 1

3. Place pieced front wrong side up. Center craft batting on wrong side of the front. Center the pieced backing on the batting with right side up. Pin through all layers.

4. Turn under raw edge of extended border ¼ inch. Fold border edge over pieced backing and pin in place, mitering corners. Press. Hand- or machine-stitch to backing.

5. Referring to photo for placement, fuse bias tape across center front strip. Make yo-yos following manufacturer's instructions. Hand-stitch yo-yos 3–5 inches apart on top of bias tape. ⊗

Source: Yo-yo maker and Quick Bias fusible bias tape #700/BGY from Clover Needlecraft Inc.

Sit With Me & Have Some Tea

Design by Connie Kauffman

This little redwork quilt is a great gift for your special friend's kitchen. Hang it from a rolling pin for a cute look. Include some favorite tea, and then sit back, relax and enjoy.

Finished size
13 x 19 inches, including tabs

Materials
• Coordinating cotton fat quarters:
    1 red/black check
    1 blue/black check
    1 black cherries print
    1 blue cherries print
    1 white solid
    1 black solid
• 3 x 6-inch scrap yellow cherries print
• 14 x 20 inches batting
• Trim:
    13 inches red narrow rickrack
    13 inches white medium rickrack
    13 inches ⅜-inch-wide white lace
    20 inches 1½-inch-wide red wire-edged ribbon
• Buttons:
    5 (½-inch) red
    4 (⅜-inch) white
    9 (⁵⁄₁₆-inch) white
• Approximately 30 red seed beads
• 4½–6½-inch-diameter white crocheted doily
• Miniature teaspoon
• 6-strand red embroidery floss
• 12-inch rolling pin
• Basic sewing supplies and equipment

Project note
For quilt to hang properly on rolling pin, the barrel of the pin needs to be at least 9 inches long. If a 12-inch rolling pin cannot be found, a hanger for the quilt can be made by cutting a 1½-inch wooden dowel to desired size and gluing large wooden beads to the ends.

Cutting
From red/black check fat quarter:
• Cut one 13½ x 2-inch strip for bottom.

• Cut two 1¾ x 5½-inch strips.

• Cut one 1¾ x 12½-inch strip. Subcut into seven 1¾ x 1¾-inch squares.

From blue/black check fat quarter:
• Cut one 2¼ x 13-inch strip.

From black cherries print fat quarter:
- Cut one 13½ x 2¾-inch strip for bottom.

From blue cherries print fat quarter:
- Cut two 1¾ x 4¼-inch strips.

- Cut one 1¾ x 12½-inch strip. Subcut into seven 1¾ x 1¾-inch squares.

From white solid fat quarter:
- Cut one 8 x 8-inch block for teapot embroidery.

- Cut one 1¾ x 5½-inch (A) strip.

- Cut one 6¾ x 1¾-inch (B) strip.

From black solid fat quarter:
- Cut two 1¾ x 16-inch strips. Subcut into 17 (1¾ x 1¾-inch) squares.

- Cut one 13½ x 16¾-inch rectangle for backing.

- Cut two 4 x 8-inch rectangles for hanging tabs.

Assembly

Use ¼-inch seam allowance unless otherwise stated. Sew right sides together. Press as you sew.

1. Transfer embroidery template onto 8 x 8-inch white block. Using 2 strands red embroidery floss and outline stitch (see stitch illustration), embroider transferred lines.

Outline Stitch

2. Cut doily in half. Immediately apply seam sealant; let dry. Sew cut edge of doily under straight embroidered line using a small zigzag stitch.

3. Lay out blocks and strips as shown in Figure 1 and sew into rows. Sew rows together to make two units (top and bottom); sew units together. Sew the 2¼ x 13-inch blue/black check strip to the right side of the unit.

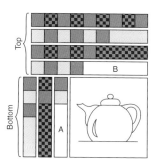

Figure 1

4. Sew red rickrack on blue/black check strip ¼ inch from seam line. Sew white rickrack ¼ inch from red rickrack. Trim ends of rickrack even with ends of strip.

5. Place the red/black check and the black cherries bottom strips with right sides together. Sandwich 13-inch length of lace between strips along one long edge. Sew strips together using a ¼-inch seam, catching edge of lace in seam (Figure 2). Trim ends of lace even with fabric strips. Press seam open and press lace over black cherries strip.

Figure 2

6. Fold yellow cherries squares diagonally twice to make triangle prairie points (Figure 3). Position the first triangle point 1½ inches from the edge of the red/black check strip. Position the second triangle beside the first, overlapping it ¼ inch. Hand-stitch the points to the red/black check strip with raw edges even.

Figure 3

7. Sew the red/black check strip to the bottom of the pieced unit. **Note:** *Take care not to catch doily in stitching.* Press strips down.

8. Fold the black 4 x 8-inch rectangles for hanging tabs in half lengthwise (2 x 8 inches) and sew long edges together. Turn right side out. Press with seams in centers of tab strips.

9. Place pieced top and backing, right sides together, on top of batting. Pin layers together. Position tabs 1½-inches in from each side on the wrong side of the quilt front. *Note: If needed, space tab position to hang over dowel or rolling pin before sewing.* Sew around edges, leaving a 3-inch opening at bottom for turning. Trim seams and clip corners. Turn right side out. Turn opening edges under and hand-stitch closed. Press.

10. Quilt as desired by stitching in the ditch along pieced strips, and around embroidered teapot. Randomly sew red seed beads to white background with black thread, knotting each bead on back of quilt.

11. Beginning at left-hand side of quilt, sew one white button in lower left corner of each red/black check strip or square across the quilt. Sew the four remaining white buttons across the red/black check bottom strip on the right-hand side of the quilt. Sew red buttons evenly spaced down the right-hand side of the blue/black check strip.

12. Tie wire-edged ribbon in a bow around the teaspoon and stitch securely in place over the triangles. ⊗

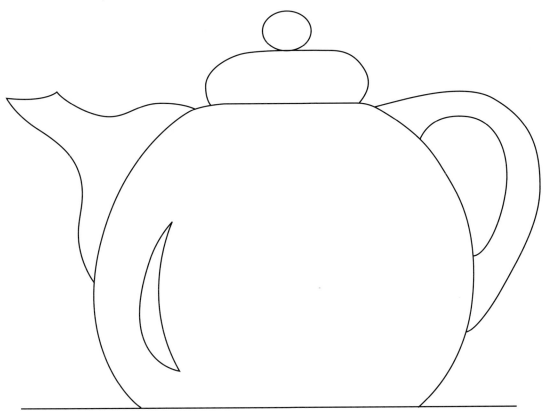

Sit With Me & Have Some Tea
Embroidery Template
Actual Size

It's All Black & White

Design by Phyllis Dobbs

Sewing an apron for the perfect hostess makes a special gift, especially when you use dramatic black-and-white fat quarters.

Finished size

Average adult

Materials

• Coordinating fat quarters:
    1 black-with-white small print
    1 white-with-black small print
    1 black-with-white large print
    1 white-with-black large print
    1 black-with-white floral lace print
• Basic sewing supplies and equipment

Cutting

Enlarge templates (page 141) for apron top and bottom flounce as indicated.

From black-with-white small print fat quarter:
 • Cut one 15¼ x 14-inch rectangle for apron bottom.

From white-with-black small print fat quarter:
 • Cut one 15¼ x 14-inch rectangle for apron bottom.

From black-with-white large print fat quarter:
 • With template face up on right side of fabric, cut one apron top.

 • Cut one 6 x 10-inch rectangle for apron pocket.

 • Cut two 2½ x 22-inch strips for apron ties.

From white-with-black large print fat quarter:
 • With template face down on right side of fabric, cut one apron top.

 • Cut one 6 x 10-inch rectangle for apron pocket.

 • Cut two 2½ x 22-inch strips for apron ties.

 • Cut one 2½ x 11½-inch strip for facing.

From black-with-white floral lace print fat quarter:
 • Use template to cut one top flounce piece on fold.

 • Use template to cut two bottom flounce pieces on fold.

Assembly

Use ½-inch seam allowance. Sew with right sides together, unless otherwise stated. Press seams as you sew.

1. Sew 15¼ x 14-inch bottom rectangles together along 14-inch edges. Sew apron tops together on center front seam. Sew top unit to bottom unit, matching seams, and alternating black and white prints.

2. Sew the two pocket rectangles together on 6-inch edges. Press seam open and press a ½-inch hem on all four sides. Topstitch top

hem only. Pin pocket to bottom unit 2 inches from upper seam, matching center seams, and alternating black and white prints. Stitch to apron on sides and bottom edges. Stitch down center seam lines to divide into two pockets.

3. Sew together long edges and one end of each 22-inch strip. Turn right side out and press flat to make ties. Hem ends of one black and one white tie for sides of apron. Set aside. The two remaining ties will be for the top.

4. Sew short edges of bottom flounces together. Sew a ¼-inch hem on bottom edge. Sew the top edge of the flounce to the bottom edge of the bottom unit.

5. Sew a ¼-inch hem on bottom and sides of top flounce. Sew a ¼-inch hem on sides and one long edge of facing piece. Pin the flounce, right side up, to the right side of the top unit with raw edges even. Referring to Figure 1, pin ties to the top unit over the flounce. Pin the facing, wrong side up, over the ties and the flounce (Figure 2).

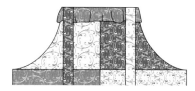

Figure 1

Figure 2

6. Sew facing, apron, ties and flounce together across top edge. Turn facing to wrong side of apron, pulling ties up. Press. Topstitch seam allowance ⅛ inch from folded edge. Hand-stitch side edges of facing to apron.

7. Press a ¼–⅜-inch hem on sides of apron and on sides of bottom flounce. Pin the end of a tie to the back of the apron bottom just below the seam line, alternating black and white prints. Stitch side seams, catching ends of ties in stitching. ⊗

Source: Blanc et Noir fabric collection by Marie Osmond from Quilting Treasures.

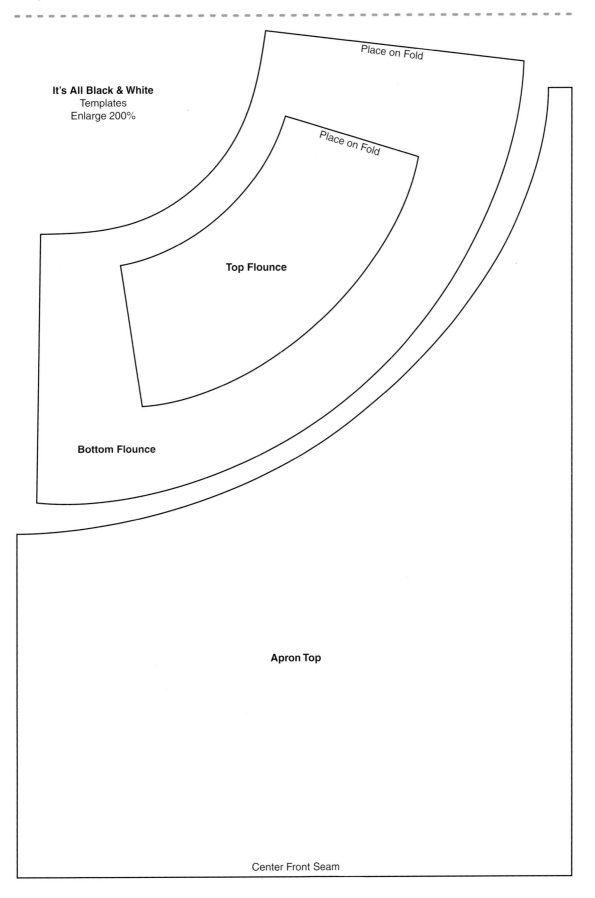

It's All Black & White
Templates
Enlarge 200%

Place on Fold

Place on Fold

Top Flounce

Bottom Flounce

Apron Top

Center Front Seam

Pink & Green Squared

Design by Rochelle Martin

Sew a pieced table runner to give as a special hostess gift, and you'll always be invited back. But keep your secret to yourself; this simple quilt pattern uses appliqué techniques instead of intricate piecing.

Finished size
36 x 12 inches

Materials
• Fat quarters:
    1 black dots
    1 green dots
    1 pink dots
• 44/45-inch-wide cotton fabric:
    ⅜ yard black-and-white print for squares and binding
    ¾ yard light green print for squares and backing
• ⅓ yard 17-inch-wide lightweight paper-backed fusible web
• Craft-size thin cotton batting
• Optional: free-motion foot
• Basic sewing supplies and equipment

Cutting
From black-dot fat quarter:
 • Cut 28 (2½-inch) squares.

From green-dot fat quarter:
 • Cut three 2¼ x 22-inch strips.

From pink-dot fat quarter:
 • Cut two 1¾ x 22-inch strips.

From black-and-white print:
 • Cut 28 (2½-inch) squares.

 • Cut three 2-inch strips the width of the fabric for binding.

From light-green print:
 • Cut 13 (4½-inch) squares.

 • Cut one 14 x 40-inch rectangle for backing.

From fusible web:
 • Cut three 2-inch strips the width of the fusible web.

 • Cut two 1½-inch strips the width of the fusible web.

Making Four-Patch Blocks

Use ¼-inch seam allowance, unless otherwise stated. Press as you sew.

1. Sew a black-and-white print 2½-inch square to a black-dot 2½-inch square (Figure 1). Press seam open. Repeat to make 28 units.

Figure 1

2. Sew two units together to make 14 Four-Patch blocks, matching center seams (Figure 2). Press seams open.

Figure 2

Adding Fancy Squares

1. Fuse the three 2-inch strips of paper-backed fusible web centered on the wrong sides of the 2¼ x 22-inch green-dot strips (Figure 3).

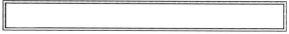

Figure 3

2. Use rotary cutter and ruler to trim each strip to 1½ x 17 inches (Figure 4). Cut 28 (1½-inch) green-dot squares from the strips (Figure 5).

Figure 4

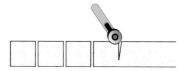

Figure 5

3. Fuse 1½-inch strips of fusible web to pink-dot strips in same manner; trim fused strips to 1 inch wide. Cut 28 (1-inch) pink-dot squares.

4. Remove paper backing from two green-dot and two pink-dot squares. Fuse to Four-Patch block as shown in Block Layout. Repeat to make 14 appliquéd blocks.

Pink & Green Squared
Block Layout

Runner Assembly

Use ¼-inch seam allowance. Sew with right sides together. Press as you sew.

1. Referring to Assembly Diagram, lay out appliquéd blocks and 4½-inch light green print squares in a 3 x 9-block format, turning some blocks as shown.

Pink & Green Squared
Assembly Diagram

2. Sew blocks into three long rows. Press seams open between blocks. Sew the three rows together, matching seams. Press open long row seams.

3. Layer table runner top, batting and backing, and baste for machine quilting. Stipple or quilt as desired in light green print blocks.

4. Quilt appliquéd blocks using a decorative stitch on edges of fused-squares, beginning by stitching around green squares (Figure 6) and then stitching around remaining edges of pink squares separately.

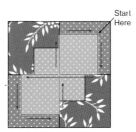

Figure 6

5. Sew edges of binding strips together; press. Fold binding lengthwise, wrong sides together and press. With right sides together and raw edges even, stitch binding to front of runner, mitering corners. Fold binding over raw edges and hand-stitch to backing. ⊗

Source: Fabric from Clothworks Textiles.

Autumn Gift Basket

Design by Carol Zentgraf

Make a reversible basket cover to fit a round basket. Our cover features summery sunflowers on one side and fall leaves on the other, but you can choose any seasons or themes that suit your fancy.

Finished size
Fits an 8-inch-diameter x 5½-inch-tall basket, or smaller

Materials
- Round 8-inch-diameter x 5½-inch-tall basket (excluding handle), or smaller
- Fat quarters:
    - 2 seasonal prints
    - 1 coordinating print for border
- 2 yards twisted-cord trim with header
- 1 yard ¼-inch-wide elastic
- Cording or zipper foot
- Basic sewing supplies and equipment

Cutting
- Measure around sides and bottom of basket from rim to rim and add 4 inches. Cut a circle this diameter from each seasonal print and border print fat quarter.

- Fold border print fat quarter circle in fourths. Draw a wavy line 3 inches from outer edge of quarter-circle (Figure 1). Cut along this line through all layers for border strip.

Figure 1

Assembly

Use ½-inch seam allowance, unless otherwise stated. Sew right sides together. Press as you sew.

1. Place one seasonal print circle right side up on flat surface. Lay border strip right side up on top of circle, aligning outer edges and pin in place. Baste outer edges in place. Sew lower edge of border strip and circle together using a short satin stitch.

2. Use a cording or zipper foot to baste twisted-cord trim to the right side of the bordered fabric circle, aligning the header with the edge of the fabric. With right sides together, sew both fabric circles together close to cord, leaving a 2-inch opening for turning. Turn right side out. Press.

3. To make elastic casing, stitch 1½ inches from the edge, leaving 2 inches unstitched directly below the outer-edge opening. Stitch a second line completely around the circle ½ inch from the first, toward the center of the circle. *Note: Instead of inserting elastic into the casing, try inserting a narrow ribbon. Place cover around basket, draw ribbon to size and tie.*

4. Thread elastic through the casing (Figure 2) with a small safety pin. Place cover on the basket and pull elastic for a snug fit. Pin elastic ends together and remove cover from basket.

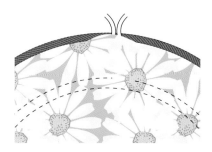

Figure 2

5. Sew elastic ends together and cut away excess ends. Stitch casing opening closed.

6. Press under seam allowances on outer edge opening and slipstitch closed. Topstitch along outer edge of border below cord trim. ⊗

Source: Fabric from Robert Kaufman Fabrics.

Sunflower Sensation

Design by Carol Zentgraf

Add interest to a pieced table runner when you embroider panels to echo the design of the main fabric for a unique gift to give to your unique friend!

Finished size

66 x 15 inches, excluding tassels

Materials

- Batik fat quarters:
    6 brown sunflower print
    2 coordinating orange print
    1 coordinating yellow print
- 8 yards ⅝-inch-wide brown gimp trim
- 2 (4-inch) brown tassels
- 3 (9 x 12-inch) sheets double-sided fusible web
- Embroidery machine with sunflower embroidery design
- Rayon machine-embroidery thread
- Tear-away stabilizer
- Optional: permanent fabric adhesive
- Basic sewing supplies and equipment

Cutting

From brown sunflower print fat quarters:

- Cut two 22 x 16-inch rectangles for center top.

- Cut four 17½ x 16-inch rectangles for backing.

From coordinating orange print fat quarters:
• Cut one 10 x 10-inch square for center top.

• Cut two 13 x 16-inch rectangles for top end panels.

From coordinating yellow print fat quarter:
• Cut two 9 x 9-inch squares for
   embroidered panels.

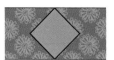

Figure 1

Figure 2

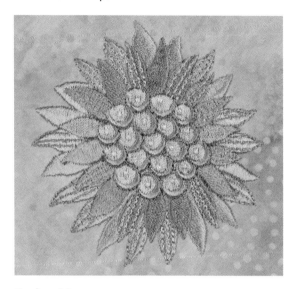

Embroidery

With stabilizer on wrong side of each yellow print
9 x 9-inch square, embroider sunflower in center.
Remove from hoop and tear away excess stabilizer.
*Note: Instead of embroidery, try a purchased
appliqué in coordinating colors.*

Assembly

Use ½-inch seam allowance. Sew with right sides
together, unless otherwise stated. Press seams
as you sew.

1. Sew short edges of 22 x 16-inch center top
   rectangles together. Sew an orange end panel
   to each end of the center. Press seams open.

2. Apply fusible web to wrong sides of orange
   center square and two embroidered yellow
   squares. Remove paper backings. Position
   orange square on point in center of runner top
   (Figure 1). Position each embroidered square
   on point in center of each end panel (Figure 2).
   Fuse in place.

3. Trim end rectangles even with outer edges of
   embroidered squares, continuing line to side
   edges to make end points (Figure 3).

Figure 3

4. Sew or glue gimp trim over all edges of center
   square, two inner edges of embroidered
   squares, and the end panel seams.

5. Sew short edges of back rectangles together,
   leaving an 8-inch opening in center of one
   seam for turning. Press seams open. Pin top and
   back together. Trim ends of back to fit top. Sew
   together along outer edges. Turn right side out
   through back seam opening. Press. Slipstitch
   opening closed.

6. Cut hanging loop of each tassel to 1½ inches.
   Apply adhesive to cut ends to prevent raveling.
   Sew or glue gimp trim around outer edges of
   runner top, inserting tassel loop ends under
   gimp at each end point. ⊗

Sources: Fabric from Robert Kaufman Fabrics; gimp trim
#I B5684CH and tassels #SM5520CH from Expo International;
Steam-A-Seam2 double-stick fusible web from The Warm
Company; rayon embroidery thread and Tear-Easy tear-away
stabilizer from Sulky of America; Fabri-Tac permanent fabric
adhesive from Beacon Adhesives.

Last-Minute Gifts

When time is of the essence, turn the pages in this chapter to find a gift you can sew in a hurry. Look for pretty and perfect pincushions for your sewing friends, a vintage-inspired fat-quarter apron for your favorite chef, or patch a pretty aromatherapy pillow filled with your favorite fragrant material. Or perhaps, a simple fabric box for chocolates is all you need. Whatever the occasion, you'll find an ideal quick gift in this chapter.

Vintage-Look Apron

Design by Chris Malone

Create a retro-chic fashion accessory by stitching this fat quarter apron in minutes. Made of reproduction fat quarters from the 1930s, this apron makes a great gift for a cook of any age.

Finished size
20 inches at front band x 20 inches long

Materials
- 5 cotton fat quarters in 1930s reproduction prints
- 1 (1⅛-inch) button
- 2⅓ yards double-fold bias tape in coordinating color
- Basic sewing supplies and equipment

Cutting
From four fat quarters:
- Cut one 12 x 19-inch rectangle for skirt panel from each. Fold each skirt panel in half lengthwise. Using scallop template (page 156), round one end of each panel.

- Cut one 5½ x 10-inch rectangle from each for patchwork tie.

From one of the four fat quarters:
- Cut one 6 x 9-inch rectangle for pocket.

From fifth fat quarter:
- Cut one 4½ x 21-inch strip for waistband.

- Cut two 5½ x 10-inch strips for waistband ties.

- Cut one 6 x 9-inch rectangle for pocket.

Assembly
Use ½-inch seam allowance unless otherwise indicated. Finish seam edges with zigzag stitches, or straight-stitch ¼ inch from raw edge and pink close to stitching. Press as you sew.

1. Sew the four skirt panels together on long edges. Press seams open and finish as desired.

2. Reinforce seams where scallops meet by stitching ⅛ inch from the edge for ½ inch on each panel (Figure 1).

Figure 1

3. Unfold bias tape. Matching raw edges of the tape with raw edges of the skirt panel, begin at the top of one outer panel and stitch on fold line to inner point of a scallop. Pivot at this point with the needle in the seam and continue down the next scallop to apply tape all around the bottom and both sides of the apron. Trim excess tape.

4. Refold the tape and bring it over the edge to the wrong side of the apron. Place the apron on a flat surface and fold a miter into each inner scallop point (Figure 2). Press well. Hand-stitch the folded edge to the wrong side of the apron, taking a few stitches in each miter.

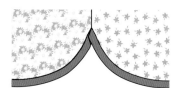

Figure 2

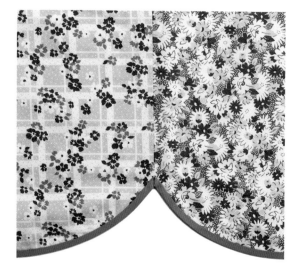

5. Sew two pocket rectangles with right sides together, using a ¼-inch seam allowance and leaving a 2-inch opening on one side. Trim corners. Turn. Fold in seam allowance and slipstitch opening closed. Press.

6. Place a pin 2½ inches down on each long side. Pin the pocket to one of the center panels approximately 4 inches down. Sew pocket in place by stitching close to the edge from one pin, across the bottom and back up to the other pin (Figure 3).

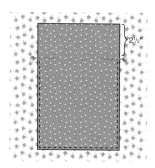

Figure 3

7. Fold pocket top down to form a contrasting flap. Sew button to flap and pocket.

8. Make two lines of gathering stitches ½ inch and ¼ inch from the top edge of the skirt. Pull threads to gather to 20 inches wide. Tie thread ends and adjust gathers evenly across.

9. Sew gathered edge to one long side of waistband, leaving ½-inch seam allowance at each end of waistband (Figure 4). On opposite long edge of waistband, press under ½ inch. Using ¼-inch seam throughout remainder of this step, sew short ends of two patchwork tie rectangles together. Repeat with remaining two rectangles. Sew one pair to each end of ties to make each tie measure 5½ x 29 inches.

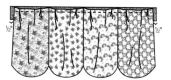

Figure 4

10. Fold each tie in half lengthwise with right sides together. Sew long edge and short end of patchwork tie together. Trim corners and turn right side out through open end. Press well. Fold a small pleat on raw end of each tie so width measures 1⅝ inches. Baste pleat in place. Matching raw edges, baste ties to ends of waistband with right sides together (Figure 5).

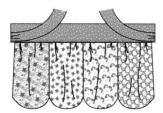

Figure 5

11. Fold waistband right sides together and sew end seams even with side hems (Figure 6).

Trim corners and turn right side out. Slipstitch the folded edge of the waistband to the inside of the apron. ⊗

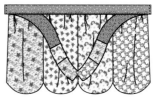

Figure 6

Sewing Tip

This apron is designed to protect the front and sides of clothing. To make it smaller to cover just the front, shorten the waistband and increase the fullness in the skirt.

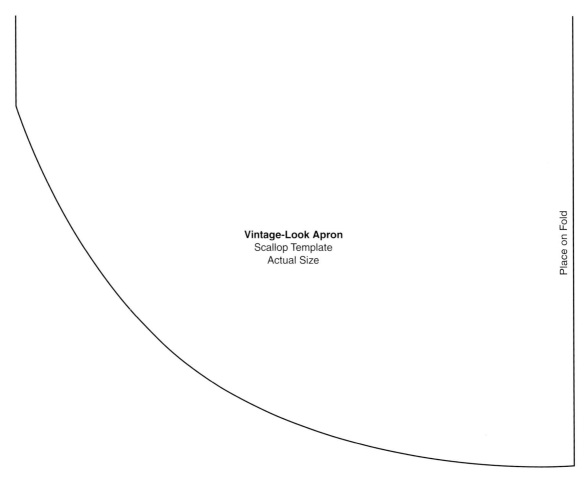

Vintage-Look Apron
Scallop Template
Actual Size

Place on Fold

Appliquéd Towel Trio

Designs by Phyllis Dobbs

Embellished kitchen or bath hand towels are simple to sew and make a great housewarming gift.

Finished size
16½ x 26½ inches

Materials
• 3 hand towels each 16½ x 25½ inches*:
    1 aqua
    1 lime green
    1 black
• Fat quarters:
    1 aqua heart print
    1 pink heart print
    1 multicolored stripe
    1 pink tonal
• Medium rickrack:
    1⅛ yards pink
    ⅝ yard aqua
• Fusible web
• 6mm round faceted glass beads:
    20 aqua
    8 green
• 2 aqua glass E beads
• Beading needle
• Basic sewing supplies and equipment

If towels vary from this size, adjust measurements accordingly throughout.

Cutting
From aqua heart print fat quarter:
• Cut a 5½ x 18½-inch rectangle for bottom trim on black towel.

• Use template (page 158) to trace two butterfly wing appliqués onto paper side of fusible web, reversing one; cut out just outside traced lines. Fuse onto wrong side of fabric; cut out on traced lines.

From pink heart print fat quarter:
• Cut a 5½ x 18½-inch rectangle for bottom trim on aqua towel.

Appliquéd Towel Trio
Templates
Actual Size

(Butterfly Body, Butterfly Wing, Flower, Heart templates)

• Use template to trace one flower appliqué onto paper side of fusible web; cut out just outside traced lines. Fuse onto wrong side of fabric; cut out on traced lines.

From multicolored stripe fat quarter:
• Cut a 5½ x 18½-inch rectangle for bottom trim on lime green towel.

From pink tonal fat quarter:
• Use template to trace one heart and one butterfly body appliqué onto paper side of fusible web; cut out just outside traced lines. Fuse onto wrong side of fabric; cut out on traced lines.

From rickrack:
• Cut two 18½-inch lengths of pink for black and lime green towels.

• Cut one 18½-inch length of aqua for aqua towel.

Assembly
1. Sew a double ¼-inch hem on one long edge and both short edges of each bottom trim piece.

2. Center trim pieces on towels 4 inches above bottom edges of towels. Turn edges to back and pin in place. Stitch ⅛ inch from raw edge.

3. Pin rickrack over stitching, turning ends to back. Sew in place.

4. Referring to photo for placement, fuse appliqués to towels; machine-appliqué edges. Using the same stitch, sew two lines for butterfly antennae.

5. Sew an aqua E bead at the tip of each antenna. Sew three aqua faceted beads on heart and three at flower center; randomly sew remaining aqua faceted beads to lime green and black towels. Sew green faceted beads randomly to aqua towel. ⊗

Sources: I Love You Zoo! fabric from Quilting Treasures; thread from Coats & Clark; faceted beads from Expo International; Steam-A-Seam2 fusible web from The Warm Company.

Crazy Patch Scented Pillow

Design by Willow Ann Sirch

Fill a pretty pillow with pleasant scents that will delight both the giver and giftee of this pretty patchwork pillow.

Finished size
8 x 6 inches

Materials
• Woven fabric fat quarters:
 1 red (A)
 1 red print (B)
 1 white patterned
• Scraps 5 decorative white patterned fabrics
• White, off-white and mauve pearl cotton or 6-strand embroidery floss
• Assorted beads, lace, appliqué
• Dried fragrant plant material or other scented filler
• Embroidery and beading needles
• Basic sewing supplies and equipment

Cutting
From red (A) fat quarter:
• Cut one 6½ x 8½-inch rectangle for pillow back.

• Cut two 3½ x 4½-inch rectangles for pillow front.

From red print (B) fat quarter:
• Cut two 3½ x 4½-inch rectangles for pillow front.

From white patterned fat quarter:
• Use template (page 163) to cut one heart for appliqué.

• Cut two 6 x 8-inch rectangles for sachet bag.

Heart Appliqué
1. Working from the right side of the heart appliqué, cover shape with small scraps of white fabrics, turning under and pinning raw edges. *Note: Each fabric raw edge should be covered by another fabric or turned under, except at outer edges of the heart.*

2. Tack the turned-under edges in place with thread. Cover each seam with a different shade of embroidery floss or pearl cotton using decorative embroidery hand or machine stitches.

3. Embellish shapes as desired with beads, lace and/or appliqué.

Assembly

Use ¼-inch seam allowance unless otherwise stated. Sew right sides together. Press seams as you sew.

1. Sew one pillow front A rectangle and one pillow front B rectangle together along short edges. Press. Repeat with remaining A and B pillow front rectangles. Sew A and B units together along long edges, alternating positions of fabrics (Figure 1). Press.

2. Center heart appliqué on pieced pillow front. Hand-appliqué in place, turning under raw edges. Work decorative embroidery stitch around outer edge.

3. Sew sachet bag rectangles together along one short and two long edges. Turn right side out. Fill with dried fragrant plant material and hand-stitch opening edge closed.

4. Sew pillow front to pillow back along one short and two long edges. Insert sachet. Turn in raw edges of front and back, and hand-stitch edges together. ⊗

Figure 1

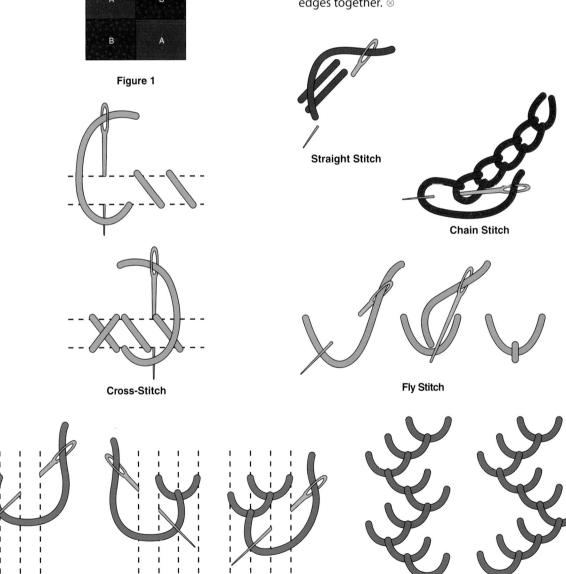

Straight Stitch

Chain Stitch

Cross-Stitch

Fly Stitch

Feather-Stitch

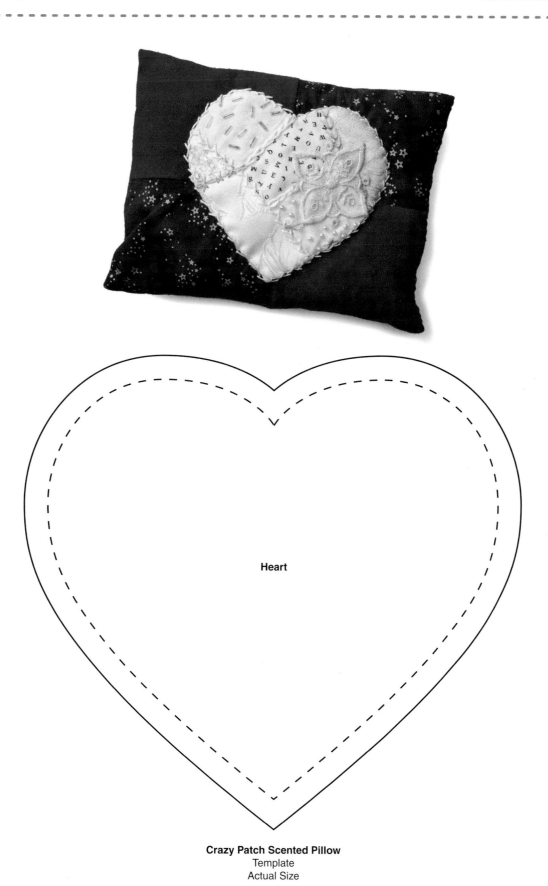

Heart

Crazy Patch Scented Pillow
Template
Actual Size

Pretty & Pink

Design by Julie Higgins

Book-jacket covers are great gifts for readers, but be sure to make one for your journal, your calendar and your personal reading. It's easy to make three coordinated book jackets by cutting them out all at once.

Finished size
5 x 7½ inches, closed; 10 x 7½ inches, opened

Materials
- 3 coordinating fat quarters
- 3 (8 x 10½-inch) pieces fusible interfacing
- Optional: 1 (10 x 12-inch) piece fusible batting*
- 10 inches ½-inch-wide ribbon for each cover
- Optional embellishments: lace, beads, appliqué, etc.
- Basic sewing supplies and equipment

Substitute this for one of the pieces of fusible interfacing if quilting one of the covers.

Cutting
From coordinating fat quarters:
Note: Stack fat quarters and cut at one time as shown in Cutting Diagram; then mix and match pieces when assembling.

- Cut one 8 x 10½-inch rectangle for outside cover.
  ***Important:** If quilting any of the covers, cut that outside cover 10 x 12 inches.*

- Cut two 8 x 3-inch rectangles for inside covers.

- Cut two 4 x 8-inch rectangles for contrast trim.

- Cut one 8 x 7-inch rectangle for inside lining.

- Optional: Cut two 10 x 2-inch strips for each set of handles desired.

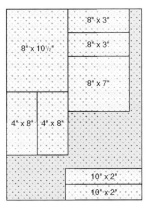

Pretty & Pink
Cutting Diagram

Assembly

Use ¼-inch seam allowance unless otherwise stated. Press as you sew.

Option: If quilting outside cover, fuse batting to wrong side of cover and quilt as desired; trim cover to 8 x 10½ inches.

1. With right sides together and 8-inch raw edges even, sew one inside cover to one contrast trim. Fold so right sides are out and raw 8-inch edges are even. Press. Repeat with each remaining inside cover and contrast trim piece.

2. Place outside cover piece right side up. If using handles, fold strips in half with right sides together. Sew together. Turn right sides out and press. Place handles on outside cover

with raw edges even and pin in place. Place ribbon length just to left or right of the center of outside cover (as you are looking at it) for bookmark (Figure 1).

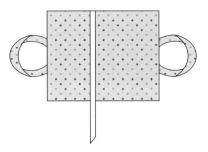

Figure 1

3. Place inside covers face down on outside cover with raw edges even and trimmed edge facedown.

4. Lay lining piece facedown over inside cover pieces, centered on outside cover with top and bottom raw edges even. ***Note: Pull ribbon bookmark up inside cover before stitching.*** Pin edges together.

5. Sew around outside edge, catching ends of handles and one end of bookmark. Clip corners. Turn right side out. Press. Embellish as desired. ⊗

Mini Gift Boxes

Design by Lynn Weglarz

This little box is the perfect size to wrap up that wonderful small treasure, or to hang on a tree, or even to use as part of your table setting. You won't be able to stop at just making one!

Finished size
2½ x 2½ x 2½ inches

Materials
• 2 coordinating fat quarters
• ¼ yard paper-backed fusible web
• ¼ yard nonwoven fusible interfacing
• Permanent fabric adhesive
• Teflon press cloth
• Optional: ribbon or cord for hanging
• Basic sewing supplies and equipment

Cutting
From coordinating fat quarters:
• Cut one 8½ x 11-inch rectangle from each fat quarter.

From paper-backed fusible web:
• Cut one 8½ x 11-inch rectangle.

From nonwoven fusible interfacing:
• Cut one 8½ x 11-inch rectangle.

Assembly

***Note:** Use a Teflon press cloth to protect iron.*

1. Fuse nonwoven fusible interfacing to the wrong side of one fat quarter rectangle.

2. Fuse paper-backed fusible web to wrong side of second fat quarter rectangle. Remove paper backing. Fuse the wrong sides of the fat quarters together, pressing on both sides. Let cool before handling.

3. Trace box template onto side of fabric you wish to be on the inside of the finished box. Cut out on traced lines. Cut slits and press fold lines as indicated on template.

4. Glue side tab inside opposite side to form sides of box; let dry. Fold under bottom flaps; tuck in box bottom.

5. Fold in flaps on top of box. If desiring to hang, attach ribbon or cord as indicated on pattern. Fold remaining flaps over and interlock slits to close. ⊗

Source: Fabri-Tac permanent fabric adhesive from Beacon Adhesives.

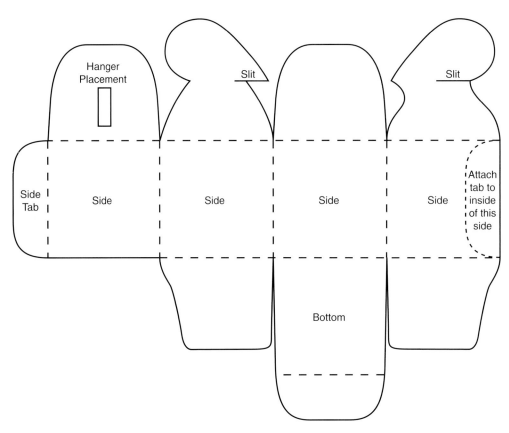

Mini Gift Boxes
Template
Enlarge 200%

Little Scrappy Pincushions

Designs by Carol Zentgraf

These fun little pincushions are a great way to use scraps from your other fat quarter projects. Add felt, cord and button accents, and then stuff them with cotton batting for quick-to-make gifts.

Finished sizes

Tomato: Approximately 10 inches in circumference x 1½ inches tall
Large Strawberry: Approximately 6 inches in circumference (at top) x 3 inches tall
Medium Strawberry: Approximately 5½ inches in circumference (at top) x 2½ inches tall
Pyramid: Approximately 3½ x 3 x 3½ inches
Pieced Square: Approximately 3½ x 3½ inches

Materials

• Scraps assorted-print fat quarters
• Scraps wool felt
• Assorted buttons
• Lightweight cord or narrow ribbon
• Cotton stuffing
• Permanent fabric adhesive
• Basic sewing supplies and equipment

Project notes

Use ¼-inch seam allowance, unless otherwise stated. Sew with right sides together. Press as you sew.

Buttons are stitched on by hand using a doubled thread.

Tomato

1. Use template (page 174) to cut eight tomato panels from fat quarter scraps and one tomato cap from wool felt scrap.

2. Sew panels together, leaving ½ inch unstitched at one end. Turn right side out and press. Stuff firmly with cotton stuffing; slipstitch open end closed.

3. Wrap cord around pincushion eight times, covering seams and twisting cords around each other at center top and bottom. Secure to center top and bottom with small dots of permanent fabric adhesive.

4. Glue tomato cap to top of pincushion. Center a button on cap and hand-sew in place, stitching up from bottom of pincushion, through buttonholes and back down, repeating for a four-hole button. Pull thread to indent top and knot thread ends securely on bottom.

Strawberry

Note: *Template is for large strawberry. Reduce 10 percent to make medium strawberry.*

1. Use templates (page 174) to cut one strawberry piece from fat quarter scrap and one strawberry cap from wool felt scrap.

2. Sew straight edges of strawberry piece together to make a cone. Turn right side out and press the seam. Stuff firmly with cotton stuffing to the top of the strawberry.

3. Using a hand-sewing needle and a double thread, run a gathering stitch around the upper edge of the strawberry. Pull thread to tightly gather the upper edge and knot thread ends to secure.

4. Sew a button to the center of the felt strawberry cap. Glue the cap to the top of the strawberry over gathers.

Pyramid

1. Use template (page 174) to cut four triangles and one 4-inch square from fat quarter scraps and two flowers from wool felt scraps.

2. Sew sides of triangles together. Sew square to bottoms of triangles, leaving an opening for turning. Turn right side out. Press. Stuff firmly with cotton stuffing. Slipstitch opening closed. Edgestitch around base of pyramid.

3. Center flowers with buttons in centers on opposite sides of pincushion. Stitch in place through button centers, stitching back and forth between the two sides and pulling the thread to indent. Knot thread securely under one flower.

Pieced Square

1. Cut four 2¼-inch squares and one 4-inch square from fat quarter scraps. Cut one flower from wool felt scrap.

2. Referring to photo, sew 2¼-inch squares together and press the seams. Sew pieced squares to the 4-inch square, right sides together, leaving an opening for turning. Turn right side out. Press. Stuff firmly with cotton stuffing. Slipstitch opening closed.

3. Wrap cord around pincushion, covering seams. Knot cord ends together at center top. Center a flower with a button center on top of pincushion. Stitch in place through the button, stitching all the way through the pincushion and back through the top, pulling the thread to indent. *Note: Stitch over cord at center bottom of pincushion to tack in place.* Knot thread under flower to secure. ⊗

Sources: Sweet Dreams Cotton Stuffing from Quilter's Dream Batting; Fabri-Tac permanent fabric adhesive from Beacon Adhesives.

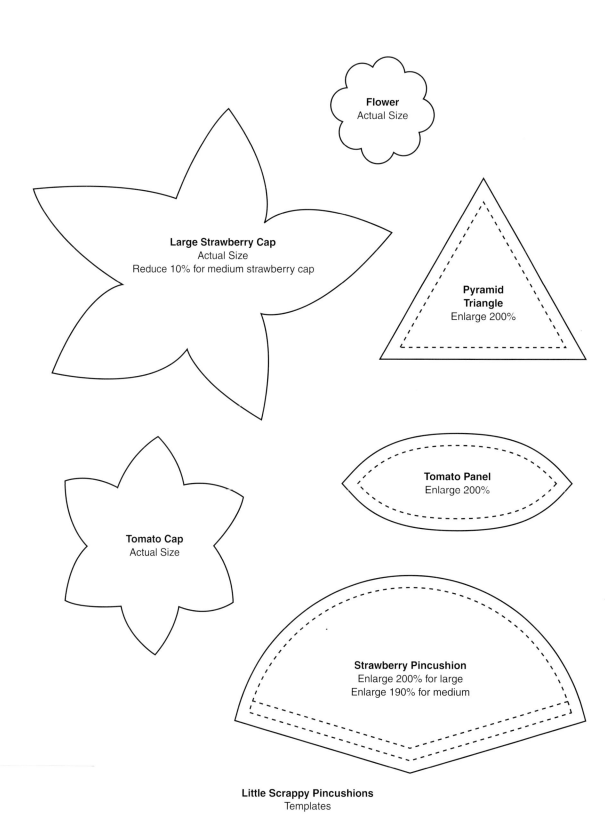

Flower
Actual Size

Large Strawberry Cap
Actual Size
Reduce 10% for medium strawberry cap

Pyramid Triangle
Enlarge 200%

Tomato Panel
Enlarge 200%

Tomato Cap
Actual Size

Strawberry Pincushion
Enlarge 200% for large
Enlarge 190% for medium

Little Scrappy Pincushions
Templates

Special Thanks

Please join us in thanking the talented designers listed below for making this book possible.

Janis Bullis
In-a-Snap Purse, 69

Holly Daniels
Patchwork Backpack, 92

Phyllis Dobbs
Poinsettia Table Runner, 128
It's All Black & White, 138
Appliquéd Towel Trio, 157

Lucy Fazely
Scrappy Rag Quilt, 59

Zoe Graul
Sew Special Gift Bags, 109

Linda Turner Griepentrog
A Day at the Zoo Quilt, 56

Pamela Hastings
Crayon Caddy, 23

Julie Higgins
Pretty & Pink, 164

Connie Kauffman
Sweet Baby Quilt, 13
Baby Announcement Board, 16
Baby Block Play Mat, 20
Pretty & Pieced, 78
Sit With Me & Have Some Tea, 134

Chris Malone
Warm & Cozy Flannel Throw, 62
Appliquéd Wine Bag, 84
Posy Cozy & Coasters, 120
Vintage-Look Apron, 153

Dorothy R. Martin
Compact Travel Bag, 104

Rochelle Martin
Pink & Green Squared, 142

Lorine Mason
Down on the Farm Gift Set, 44

Patsy Moreland
Summer Delight Runner, 131

Missy Shepler
On the Go Bag, 96
Petite Purses, 100

Willow Ann Sirch
A Stitch in Time Tote, 81
Sewing Circle Etui, 88
Crazy Patch Scented Pillow, 161

Cheryl Stranges
Dots, Flowers & Bows, 30

Lisa Swenson Ruble
Hugs & Kisses Baby Woobie, 26

Carolyn Vagts
Stitched With Love Quilt & Tote, 7
Color My World, 36
Coffee, Tea or Me? 115

Lynn Weglarz
Cookie Tray Set, 124
Mini Gift Boxes, 167

Sheila Zent
A Gift for Her, 74

Carol Zentgraf
Yo-Yo Puppy, 41
Windmill Twin Quilt, 50
It's Popping Up Pillows! 53
Tumbling Stripes Throw, 65
Autumn Gift Basket, 146
Sunflower Sensation, 149
Little Scrappy Pincushions, 170

Basic Sewing Supplies & Equipment

- Sewing machine and matching thread
- Serger, if desired
- Scissors of various sizes, including pinking shears
- Rotary cutter(s), mats and straightedges
- Pattern tracing paper or cloth
- Pressing tools such as sleeve rolls, tailor's ham and pressing boards
- Pressing equipment, including ironing board and iron; press cloths

- Straight pins and pin cushion
- Measuring tools, tape measures and rulers
- Marking pens (either air- or water-soluble) or tailor's chalk
- Spray adhesive (temporary)
- Hand-sewing needles and thimble
- Point turners
- Seam sealant
- Seam ripper

Sewing Sources

The following companies provided fabric and/or supplies for projects in this book. If you are unable to locate a product locally, contact the manufacturers listed below for the closest retail or mail-order source.

Adhesive Products Inc.
(510) 526-7616
www.adhesiveproducts
inc.com

Beacon Adhesives Inc.
(914) 699-3405
www.beaconcreates.com

Benartex
(212) 840-3250
www.benartex.com

Clothworks Textiles
(800) 874-0541
www.clothworkstextiles.com

Clover Needlecraft Inc.
(800) 233-1703
www.clover-usa.com

Coats & Clark
(800) 648-1479
www.coatsandclark.com

Expo International
(800) 542-4367
www.expointl.com.

Fairfield Processing
(800) 980-8000
www.poly-fil.com

G Street Fabrics
(301) 231-8998
www.gstreetfabrics.com

Ghee's
(318) 226-1701
www.ghees.com

Hobbs Bonded Fibers
(800) 433-3357
www.hobbsbonded
fibers.com

Hoffman California Fabrics
(800) 547-0100
www.hoffmanfabrics.com

Husqvarna Viking
(440) 808-6550
www.husqvarnaviking.com

JHB International Inc.
(800) 525-9007
www.buttons.com

Kandi Corp.
(800) 985-2634
www.kandicorp.com

Martha Pullen
(800) 547-4176
www.marthapullen.com

Michael Miller Fabrics
(212) 704-0774
www.michaelmiller
fabrics.com

Moda Fabrics
(800) 527-9447
www.unitednotions.com/
wtb.nsf/wtb_us

Newark Dressmaker Supply
(800) 736-6783
www.newarkdress.com

Pellon Consumer Products
(877) 817-0944
www.shoppellon.com

Prym Consumer USA Inc.
www.prymdritz.com

Quilters Dream Batting
(888) 268-8664
www.quiltersdream
batting.com

Quilting Treasures
(800) 876-2756
www.quiltingtreasures.com

Robert Kaufman Fabrics
(800) 877-2066
www.robertkaufman.com

Sulky of America
(800) 874-4115
www.sulky.com

Therm O Web
(800) 323-0799
www.thermoweb.com

The Warm Company
(425) 248-2424
www.warmcompany.com

This book is enhanced by the product support of tools and supplies, provided to our designers by the vendors listed on this page.